TO KNOW HIM

TO KNOW HIM

BEYOND RELIGION
WAITS A RELATIONSHIP THAT
WILL CHANGE YOUR LIFE

Gloria Copeland

New York   Boston   Nashville

Unless otherwise noted, Scriptures are taken from the King James Version of the Bible.

Scriptures marked AMP are taken from the Amplified® Bible. Copyright © 1954, 1962, 1965, 1987 by The Lockman Foundation. Used by permission.

Scriptures noted NJV are taken from the HOLY BIBLE: NEW INTERNATIONAL VERSION®. Copyright © 1973, 1978, 1984 by international Bible Society. Used by permission of Zondervan Publishing House. All rights reserved.

Scriptures noted TLB are taken from *The Living Bible*, copyright © 1971. Used by permission of Tyndale House Publishers, Inc., Wheaton, Illinois 60189. All rights reserved.

Scriptures marked WEYMOUTH are taken from The New Testament in Modern Speech by Richard Francis Weymouth. Copyright © 1996 by Kenneth Copeland Publications. Used by permission.

Scriptures noted NASB are taken from the New American Standard Bible®. Copyright © 1960, 1962, 1963, 1968, 1972, 1975, 1977, 1995 by The Lockman Foundation. Used by permission.

Originally published by Kenneth Copeland Ministries as *Living Contact* (1996) and as *Living Contact: The Secret to Overcoming Life* (2002). Previously published in 2005 by Harrison House as *To Know Him*.

The FaithWords edition is published by arrangement with Harrison House, Inc., Tulsa, Oklahoma.

FaithWords
Hachette Book Group
1290 Avenue of the Americas
New York, NY 10104

www.faithwords.com

The Hachette Speakers Bureau provides a wide range of authors for speaking events. To find out more, go to www.hachettespeakersbureau.com or call (866) 376-6591.

The publisher is not responsible for websites (or their content) that are not owned by the publisher.

Printed in the United States of America

First FaithWords Edition: September 2008

11

FaithWords is a division of Hachette Book Group, Inc. The FaithWords name and logo are trademarks of Hachette Book Group, Inc.

Library of Congress Cataloging-in-Publication Data

Copeland, Gloria.
To know Him : beyond religion waits a relationship that will change your life / Gloria Copeland.—1st FaithWords ed.
    p.   cm.
ISBN-13: 978-0-446-51124-7
ISBN-10: 0-446-51124-2
1. Spirituality. I. Title.
BV4501.3.C675 2008
248.4—dc22
2007047216

Contents

Contents

Preface

I believe we are in the last of the last days. It's time to move into a closeness with God where you live separated unto Him and obey Him in all the areas of your life. Jesus said, "If you abide in Me and My words abide in you, ask what you will and it will be done." (See John 15:7.) That's living in fellowship with God. And it produces a great reward.

If you want to know God, you will have to spend time with Him. Knowing Him requires a lifestyle of talking to Him and communing with Him. That's living contact. It's listening to Him and obeying what you hear in your heart and what you see in the written Word. Learning to live in the place where God can talk to you at any moment and you hear and obey is the secret to living an overcoming life.

To know Him should be, without question, the number one priority in every person's life. It is the key that opens every door.

Daily communion with God—being intimate with Him— strengthens you and undergirds your faith. It's the way love works. A living connection with God produces the anointing that enables us to lay hold of all the wonderful things God has provided for us through Jesus Christ.

What you will have in your life tomorrow will be determined by what is in your heart today. So, when you fill your heart with the Word and the voice of God, you will abide in Him every day and feast your heart on His promises and His presence, and your future will be one of joy and prosperity, healing and health. Instead of chasing after the blessings of God, you'll find they're chasing you and overtaking you at every turn! Understanding this message has changed my life forever.

Gloria Copeland

TO KNOW HIM

First Things First

During my years of walking with the Lord, He has taught me many wonderful things. He has taught me about faith and righteousness, healing and prosperity. He has taught me so many vital truths from His Word for which I am very grateful. And He's teaching me more every day.

Yet, if you were to ask me to name the most important principle of Christian living that I've learned, I could answer you without hesitation.

It is the secret of maintaining a living connection with God.

Staying in daily communion with Him is, without question, the number one priority of the Christian life. It is the key that opens every door to this life and the next.

If we don't really know God, it doesn't matter how much information we have about Him. We can be full of knowledge about faith. We can understand how it comes, what it does and how to release it. We can study about love until we have memorized every love scripture in the Bible. We can know the steps to healing and prosperity backward and forward. But we won't have the *momentum* to put those things into action unless we spend time with God and maintain a living connection with Him.

When all is said and done, it's not what we know that counts; it's what we actually do. And without vital, continual union with God, we won't be spiritually strong enough to do what we know to do! As Philippians 2:12–13 says:

> *Therefore, my dear ones, as you have always obeyed [my suggestions], so now, not only [with the enthusiasm you would show] in my presence but much more because I am absent, work out (cultivate, carry out to the goal, and fully complete) your own salvation with reverence and awe and trembling (selfdistrust, with serious caution, tenderness of conscience, watchfulness against temptation, timidly shrinking from whatever might offend God and discredit the name of Christ). [Not in your own strength] for it is God who is all the while effectually at work in you [energizing and creating in you the power and desire], both to will and to work for His good pleasure and satisfaction and delight.* (AMP)

It's amazing how many Christians don't realize that. They rush around trying to do things in their own strength. They run from one good thing to the next, trying to serve the Lord. But because they don't maintain a living connection with God, they end up tired, frustrated and defeated.

They are like Martha on the day Jesus ministered in her home. Instead of sitting at Jesus' feet and listening to Him teach the Word as her sister, Mary, was doing, Luke 10:40–42 says:

But Martha [overly occupied and too busy] was dis-
tracted with much serving; and she came up to Him and said,
Lord, is it nothing to You that my sister has left me to serve
alone? Tell her then to help me [to lend a hand and do her
part along with me]! But the Lord replied to her by saying,
Martha, Martha, you are anxious and troubled about many
things; There is need of only one.... Mary has chosen the
good portion [that which is to her advantage], which shall
not be taken away from her. (Luke 10:40–42, AMP)

An Awesome Privilege

As you can see from Mary's example, there is nothing complicated
about establishing a living connection with Jesus. Even the new-
est believer can do it. Abiding with God is simply fellowshiping
with Him. It's staying in touch with Him. It's talking to Him and
listening to Him. It's setting aside the distractions and demands of
life and taking the time to commune with Him in His Word and
in prayer.

Some people say, "Well, I'd like to do that, but my schedule just
won't permit it."

Actually, I don't believe they would say that if they realized
what an awesome privilege it is to fellowship with Almighty God.
If they had a genuine revelation of the fact that the Creator and
Ruler of the entire universe has made Himself available to person-
ally meet with them every day, they would change their schedules.
They would find some way to make time for Him.

Think about what an amazing opportunity it is to personally

commune with God. Adam and Eve had that opportunity in the Garden of Eden. God would come and walk with them in the cool of the day. But then they sinned and lost their ability to have that kind of contact with God. They died spiritually, so they were unable to respond to Him as they once had done.

When God came calling for them, instead of standing righteous and unashamed in His presence, they ran and hid because they were full of shame and condemnation.

What a loss! What a tragedy that was!

Because of their sin, for 4,000 years afterward, mankind was locked out of the presence of God. Even the Israelites—God's special people—were unable to fellowship freely with Him. When they needed divine help or healing, they had to go to the priest. And though the priest had the anointing of God on him, even he couldn't go boldly into God's presence whenever he wanted. Only the high priest could go behind the thick veil of the temple into the Holy of Holies where the presence of God dwelt. And he could only go there once a year with great precaution and always with the blood of an animal to atone for his sin as well as for the sins of the people.

But hallelujah, when Jesus went to the cross for us, all that changed! He paid the price for our sins. He shed His own blood not just to atone for sin, but to remit it. His sacrifice of Himself for us restored man's lost fellowship with God when we choose Him as our Lord and Savior.

Now as born-again believers, we "have full freedom and confidence to enter into the [Holy of] Holies [by the power and virtue] in the blood of Jesus" (Hebrews 10:19, AMP). God is accessible to us once again. He has made us new creations and put His own

Spirit inside us so that we ourselves can be temples of the living God. He has given us His righteousness so that instead of hiding from the presence of God, we can "come boldly unto the throne of grace, that we may obtain mercy, and find grace to help in time of need" (Hebrews 4:16).

My, what a privileged people we are! We can commune with Him any time of the day or night.

God has flung open to us the door of fellowship. He has said, "I'm here for you. Just draw near to Me and I'll draw near to you. I'll give you the wisdom you need. I'll strengthen you and equip you and help you in every area of your life."

Yet how many Christians are daily taking advantage of this wonderful privilege? Too few. They're too busy with the affairs of life to take the time for Him.

"Well, Gloria," you might say, "considering how much we have to do these days, that's understandable."

Is it? Think about it from another perspective for a moment, and I think you'll change your mind.

Suppose you wake up one morning, walk into your kitchen and Jesus is sitting at the table. "Well, Jesus!" you would say with surprise. "I'm thrilled You came by. I've really been wanting to see You. I have some serious problems and I need Your help. I wish I had time to talk to You about them right now, but I have to run. I'm having lunch downtown and I have to take care of some business. Maybe we'll have time to talk awhile when I come home tonight."

When you arrive home, your son has a Little League game, so you rush out the door saying, "I'm sorry, Jesus. I have to go to the game right now. We'll spend a few minutes together before I go to bed tonight, OK?"

But when you return from the Little League game, you are so tired. You think, *I just need to watch a little television to relax.* Then you fall asleep in front of the television, while Jesus continues to sit and wait for you at your kitchen table. Finally, the day has slipped completely away, and you have missed your opportunity to be with Him.

Of course, you probably think you would never do such a thing. If Jesus physically came to your house, you'd stop everything just to be with Him. Yet, when you understand how real the spirit realm is, when you fully realize that His precious Holy Spirit is right there inside you, waiting for you day after day, you'll see that it's just as foolish to neglect your daily fellowship with Him in the Word and in prayer as it would be to leave Jesus sitting alone at your kitchen table.

It is my prayer that as you read this book, the Holy Spirit will give you a deeper revelation of that truth and that He will strengthen you in your commitment to put first things first and make a living connection with Jesus every day.

I know from experience, it will forever change your life.

CHAPTER 2

Living to Know Him

Of course, even after you make Jesus the Lord of your life, it takes more than a few casual contacts with God to learn how to be an overcomer. It takes a lifestyle of communing with Him and spending time with Him. If we truly want to see what God can do, we can't be content to run to Him only in the hard times or when we're in desperate need. We can't be satisfied just to work Him into our schedules when it's convenient. We must build our schedules around our time with Him. We must seek God in prayer and the Word every single day—when things are hard and when they're easy, in good times and in bad.

If you think about it, it's just plain smart.

After all, God is the only One who has all the answers. He knows where you need to go in life and how to get you there. He has the solution for every problem. He has the master plan for your life!

Generally, He won't run you down to get your attention so He can give you those solutions. No, He will wait for you to do your part. What is your part? To draw near to Him. If you'll do that, He'll draw near to you in return. He gave us His Word on it: "Draw nigh to God, and he will draw nigh to you" (James 4:8). Hebrews 10:22 says, "Let us draw near with a true heart in full assurance of faith...."

When you call on God, you will never be answered by "voice mail." You'll never hear a recording, as you do so often when you make phone calls these days. You'll never hear Him say, "Hello, this is God. I'm away from the throne right now. Please leave a message and I'll return your call as soon as I can."

No, He is always there for you. If you feel like He hasn't been talking to you lately, you had better check up on yourself and see how much you've been talking to Him. If you don't feel like He's been paying enough attention to you, then start paying more attention to Him!

The moment you turn to God, He'll be there for you. Don't wait until trouble comes to turn to Him. Develop a lifestyle of fellowshiping with God and becoming more intimately acquainted with Him. Fellowship with the Lord daily, even when things are going well, and you will avoid most trouble. If trouble does come, you'll be spiritually strong enough to overcome it. Jesus said that in the world we will have tribulation. (See John 16:33.) It doesn't matter who you are or how rich or well educated you are or even how much faith you have. In this life you will face some tests and trials. The devil is roaming around this earth seeking someone to steal from, kill and destroy, and you will have to deal with him. So you'd better be ready to fight the good fight of faith at any time. A good fight is a fight you win! In the same verse, Jesus, our Champion and Savior, also said, "I have overcome the world." When we stay in vital union with Him, we will always have victory, even in a time of trouble.

You may not be in a desperate situation today, but as long as you live on this earth, you will need your faith. This is a crazy world, and this is a critical hour. If you want to survive in it successfully, you'll have to latch onto the power of God and walk in His ways.

This is not the time to be a lukewarm, lazy Christian. This is the time to be on fire for God, because nothing else will work. The closer we approach the end of this age, the less dependable natural things will become. In the days ahead, there will be more diseases that medicine can't cure. There will be financial problems and social problems that men can't solve.

In times like these there is just one sure source of supply and that's God. And only by letting Him be God in our lives will we be able to walk through these troubled times in triumph. Only by making Him number one and putting time with Him ahead of ourselves, our families, our careers and everything else will we have victory in our lives.

It has surprised some people to hear me say that. They think we teach that you won't have any problems if you live by faith. But, if that's what they think, they obviously have never listened to us, because we don't say you won't have any problems. We just say that when the problems come, you'll have an answer for them.

Everyone has trouble, sinners and saints alike. The difference is that when a Bible-believing, Spirit-filled child of God faces trouble, he doesn't face it alone. God says, "I will be with him in trouble; I will deliver him, and honour him" (Psalm 91:15).

Who is with you in trouble makes the difference. If your only help is your own natural strength and resources, you might come out of that trouble all right or you might not. But if God is with you, you can be sure you'll come out victorious!

The Victory Is in Your Heart

It is important that you make it your priority to spend time in prayer and in the Word *during good times*. Then you can be sure that in the hard places you'll be so accustomed to looking to Him, you won't let the feelings or circumstances of the moment pull you away from your dependency on Him. You want to be strong in your communion with God so that you have the assurance and the power to cast down the fears and imaginations and threats of the devil that come during times of trouble.

You also want to daily develop your ability to hear from Him so that when you're in a desperate place, you'll be able to hear His voice.

Just one word from God can change your whole situation in a moment. Ken and I have experienced that again and again through the years. We've been in times of deep trouble. We've faced situations that looked impossible. But God has always helped us and brought us through in victory.

On one particular occasion, we fell behind on our television bills and found ourselves almost $6 million in the red. (That might not seem like much money to you, but to us it was serious! We aren't used to owing anybody anything. Everything in our ministry—including all of our buildings—is debt free.) With every day that passed, those television bills kept rolling in, and we just kept falling further behind. Month after month went by with no improvement. Naturally speaking, we made every adjustment we knew to make. Yet, nothing seemed to help.

So, Ken and I just kept walking by faith, staying in contact with God day after day in prayer and in the Word. There were times when even that didn't appear to be making any difference. But we live by faith and not by sight, so when we would become tired and want to faint, we would just pick ourselves up and feed our faith with God's Word. We would get back to that place of faith where He could sustain us by His strength and power.

Then one day something happened inside of us. The Spirit of God moved in our hearts and we received the breakthrough. Aggressive faith took hold, and despite the fact that the bills were still unpaid, we knew in our hearts the money we needed was ours.

Sure enough, within just a few months, that impossible-looking debt was paid!

Once we had the victory on the inside, the circumstances had to bow their knee, because victory on the inside always brings victory on the outside. That's a spiritual fact. Once you lay hold of deliverance, healing or prosperity in your heart, all the devils in hell can't stop it from coming to pass in your life.

We stayed current for about ten years and the same thing happened again. This time, we had experience to help us. We were like David when he stood before Goliath. We remembered the lion and the bear. We remembered how God had delivered us the last time. We took the high ground of faith again. "The victory that overcometh the world, even our faith" brought us out again (1 John 5:4)!

Daily communion with God is absolutely vital to your success—because victory is won first in the heart and then in the circumstances.

CHAPTER 3

Surprise! God Is Good—Not Angry

In building a day-to-day relationship with God, it's important to know that He loves you and only has good in mind for you. Your picture of God has everything to do with your relationship to Him. A wrong picture produces a wrong relationship.

The wrong picture has been painted for thousands of years. All over the world, confused and misguided people have offered up sacrifices, trying to appease one "angry god" or another. It may surprise you to discover that even today people are still doing things to try to turn what they think is God's anger from them. And this is happening not just in remote, primitive corners of the earth. In fact, many Christians fall into a similar trap. I hear it all too frequently.

People talk as if the God we serve is angry and vengeful. They speak as if God is their problem. If anything bad happens to them, they're sure God is thumping them on the head because they got out of line; or that He is bringing heartache into their lives "to teach them something."

Far too many church-going people are "serving God" sacrificially because they believe He is basically mad at them and must be appeased. It always saddens me to hear God's people talk this way because it is so far from the truth. It's no wonder they have trouble receiving from God! They have not developed their faith. If only they would look to His Word and discover the good news they would see the right picture.

Jehovah the Good

Everything we receive from God, we receive by faith. And nothing is more faith building than discovering (or being reminded) that our heavenly Father is good. Absolute good!

One of my favorite reminders is found throughout the Old Testament in the very name of God. In fact, in 2 Chronicles 30:18, the words translated "the good Lord" in English are actually in the original Hebrew title for God: "Jehovah the Good."

I'm here to tell you from experience that the more you come to know Jehovah the Good, the easier it is for you to receive all the good things He promises you in His Word. After all, 1 John 3:21-22 tells us: "Beloved, if our heart condemn us not, then have we confidence toward God. And whatsoever we ask, we receive of him...."

Many of God's people never have any confidence before Him because they've never received the revelation of His goodness. When you know someone is good and kind, you trust him and have confidence when you approach him for something you need.

We see another great picture of "Jehovah the Good" in Psalm 145:5-9:

> *I will speak of the glorious honour of thy majesty, and of thy wondrous works. And men shall speak of the might of thy terrible acts: and I will declare thy greatness. They shall*

abundantly utter the memory of thy great goodness, and
shall sing of thy righteousness. The Lord is gracious, and full
of compassion; slow to anger, and of great mercy. The Lord
is good to all: and his tender mercies are over all his works.

I want everyone I meet to know that "the Lord is gracious and full of compassion." *Gracious* means "disposed to show favors." *Compassion* is "an eager yearning to do good." That's the God I've come to know—the One who is "good to all."

My God has vast treasure houses of His goodness stored up for us, and His greatest desire is to pour it out in our lives!

That's not just an exciting thought. That's what the Bible teaches.

Psalm 31:19 says, "Oh how great is thy goodness, which thou hast laid up for them that fear thee; which thou hast wrought for them that trust in thee before the sons of men!" A Hebrew translation says God has "treasured" so much goodness for those who honor and reverence Him—so much goodness that others will be able to see it.

The Great One Within

Now I want you to see another confidence-building aspect of the goodness of God.

When Ken and I first came into the things of God, there was a scripture that literally became a lifesaver for us. Whenever it seemed we were about to be overwhelmed by circumstances or pressure, we would run to this verse and shore up our faith and trust: "Ye are of God, little children, and have overcome them: because greater is he that is in you, than he that is in the world" (1 John 4:4).

What a wonderful, saving scripture this has been for us! Whenever it seemed the manifestation of God's promise was slow in coming...whenever it seemed that there was no way we were going to win...we would turn to this truth about the "Greater One" living within us and we would receive the strength to stand. This truth is a wonderful place to run when it looks like all is lost.

Of course, all is never lost if you will refuse to quit believing and trusting God. This is a vital necessity for enjoying victory that we have learned. If you don't quit believing and trusting, victory is assured.

I also like what the next two verses say: "They are of the world: therefore speak they of the world, and the world heareth them. We are of God: he that knoweth God heareth us; he that is not of God heareth not us" (1 John 4:5–6).

The good news from the verses above is that we are not of the world. We are "of God," and that is why we can be sure that "God heareth us."

We have the peace and confidence that come from knowing that the Greater One is living within us. He is greater than anyone or anything in the world and He hears us when we speak. That confidence grows even stronger as we receive revelation of His goodness.

Love Never Fails

One of the best ways to get the revelation of God's goodness is to discover more about His love for you.

It's important to note that the Bible never explicitly says, "God is power," although He certainly is awesomely powerful. It never says, "God is truth," although we know He is the source of all truth and can never lie. But the Bible does tell us in 1 John 4:8 that "God is love."

The Word says so again a few verses later: "And we have come to know and have believed the love which God has for us. *God is love,* and the one who abides in love abides in God, and God abides in him. By this, love is perfected with us, that we may have confidence in the day of judgment; because as He is, so also are we in this world" (verses 16–17, *New American Standard*).

This Scripture is saying to us that because we've been born of *His* Spirit, we can love with *His* love and be like Him.

Notice that these verses talk about "believing" the love God has for you. It tells us that believing in God's love gives you "confidence" before Him. If you don't believe the love of God, you won't have confidence in Him to help you when you need it. You won't have confidence in Him to see you through hard days or difficult situations.

Because God is love, He wants only the best for us. You really begin to understand the depth of that truth when you look at the Bible's definition of "love" in 1 Corinthians 13.

We usually apply these verses to ourselves, using them as a standard by which we can compare our behavior and check our love walk. But since "God is love," we can also look at these verses and get a clearer picture of how God is going to respond to us.

Love endures long and is patient and kind; love never is envious nor boils over with jealousy, is not boastful or vainglorious, does not display itself haughtily.... Love bears up under anything and everything that comes, is ever ready to believe the best of every person, its hopes are fadeless under

*all circumstances, and it endures everything [without weak-
ening]. Love never fails [never fades out or becomes obso-
lete or comes to an end].* (1 Corinthians 13:4, 7–8, AMP)

Since God *is* love, then He must be perfect and complete in loving us in the way described in these verses. God "endures long"
with you. He is "patient" with you and "kind" to you. God is "ever
ready to believe the best" about you.

"Love never fails." And since God *is* love, that means He will
never fail you.

Doesn't getting a revelation of God's love and faithfulness have
a powerful impact on your heart? Do you feel your confidence
in His goodness rising as you read about His love? I know mine
does.

If you will dare to believe the Word of God and see the true
picture of God, your confidence in Him will soar. As it does, so
will your ability to receive from Him. Confidence in God is a definition of faith.

"Therefore, do not throw away your confidence, which has a
great reward. For you have need of endurance, so that when you
have done the will of God, you may receive what was promised"
(Hebrews 10:35–36 NASB).

Don't throw away your confidence. Increase it by keeping the
love and goodness of God in your heart and in your mouth.

Always remember: you're not trying to appease an angry God!
You can have peace in your heart and mind because you serve a
heavenly Father who loves and cherishes you. When you know
that, you'll want to spend time with Him every day. You will abide
in Him with joy.

CHAPTER 4

Abiding in the Vine

In John 15, Jesus reveals to us just how important abiding in Him truly is. He considered it such a crucial matter that He spoke to His disciples strongly about it just before He went to the cross. Therefore, we should pay serious attention to the words He said.

You may have read them many times before, but take a moment and read them again carefully as if you were reading them for the first time.

I am the true vine, and my Father is the husbandman. Every branch in me that beareth not fruit he taketh away: and every branch that beareth fruit, he purgeth it, that it may bring forth more fruit. Now ye are clean through the word which I have spoken unto you. Abide in me, and I in you. As the branch cannot bear fruit of itself, except it abide in the vine; no more can ye, except ye abide in me. I am the vine, ye are the branches: He that abideth in me, and I in him, the same bringeth forth much fruit: for without me ye can do nothing. If a man abide not in me, he is cast forth as a branch, and is withered; and men gather them, and cast

them into the fire, and they are burned. If ye abide in me,
and my words abide in you, ye shall ask what ye will, and it
shall be done unto you. Herein is my Father glorified, that
ye bear much fruit... (John 15:1–8)

To understand what Jesus was saying there, you must realize
that He was not just instructing us to enjoy occasional times of
fellowship with Him. He was telling us to abide in Him. The word
abide has a sense of permanency about it. It doesn't mean "to
come in and go out." It refers to the place where you remain and
dwell continually.

When Ken and I travel, we might stay in a hotel for a week. We
live there temporarily, but we don't abide there. We abide in our
home in Fort Worth, Texas. That's where all our belongings are.
That's where we continually live. That's our abode!

By the same token, when Jesus said, "Abide in me," He wasn't
saying, "Live in fellowship with Me one day and with the world the
next." He wasn't talking about a sporadic or temporary arrangement. He was instructing us to make that place of dependency and
communion with Him our permanent dwelling place.

And He immediately told us why we must do that. It's because
if we don't, we won't be able to produce results in our lives. If
we're not continually walking with Him and talking with Him—
continually spending time in His Word and listening for the
Spirit's direction on the inside—spiritually we won't be able to
accomplish anything!

Contrary to what many people seem to think, you cannot live
from Sunday to Sunday—fellowshiping with the Lord at church
once a week and ignoring Him the rest of the time—and still live

a successful Christian life. Jesus was quite clear about that. Read again what He said in John 15:6: "If a man abide not in me, he is cast forth as a branch, and is withered; and men gather them, and cast them into the fire, and they are burned."

It doesn't matter how close a branch is to a vine. The moment the branch is broken from it, it will begin to die. You can lay the branch right next to the vine, but if the union has been broken, there will be no life flow. There will be no sap flowing from the vine into the branch—no life flowing.

The same is true for us when we become too busy to spend time with God in prayer and in His Word. When we become preoccupied with natural, earthly things and disconnect from communion with Him, we immediately begin to wither.

To *wither* is "to shrivel; to lose or cause to lose energy, force or freshness." That's a vivid picture of what happens to us when we aren't in vital contact and living union with the Lord. We still belong to Him. We still have His life within us, but His energy is not flowing through us. We can't produce anything beyond the natural. Even though we are born of the Spirit to live in the supernatural power of the living God, we lose our capacity for spiritual action. We may know what to do, but we find ourselves failing to do it. We lose our desire to do the work God has called us to do. And even those things we are able to do become dry and spiritless.

Have you ever been to a church and heard an old, dead sermon? When you walked out of that service you might have said, "My goodness, that was dry!" The reason it was dry was that it didn't flow from a heart in union with the living God.

I'm not saying the preacher was in sin or had backslidden. On the contrary, he may have spent years fellowshiping with God. But a living connection with God can't be stored up. It's like the manna the children of Israel ate in the wilderness: It must be fresh every day.

I don't care how great an orator you may be; you can't preach a good sermon if you aren't living in union and communion with the Lord. People try all the time. They'll work hard to come up with eloquent phrases and great ideas. They might even buy books and preach sermons that were written by anointed men or women of God. But those sermons won't be as good when a dried up preacher preaches them, because if he hasn't had fellowship with God, there won't be any life behind his words.

Of course, preachers aren't the only ones who dry up when they don't maintain daily communion with God. Anyone who fails to abide in Jesus will be spiritually barren. Jesus made that very plain. He didn't stutter. He just said straight out that unless we abide in Him, we "can do nothing."

I'm not sure very many Christians believe that. If they did, they wouldn't be so prone to skipping their times with God.

John 15:4–5 says, "Abide in me, and I in you. As the branch cannot bear fruit of itself except it abide in the vine; no more can ye, except ye abide in me. I am the vine, ye are the branches: He that abideth in me, and I in him, the same bringeth forth much fruit: for without me ye can do nothing." If Christians really believed this, instead of thinking, *I'm too busy to take time to pray and read the Word today*, they'd think, *My schedule is so packed, I'd better get up early so I can spend some extra time with God! I can't afford to be a spiritual "do-nothing" today. I need to produce a lot of fruit!*

We all need to adopt that kind of attitude. We need to acknowledge that we can't do anything on our own. But we shouldn't be stuck there. We shouldn't go around talking about how helpless we are without Jesus. That's not productive. We need to say, "Without Him I can do nothing, but, praise God, I'm not without Him! I'm with Him, and I can do all things through Him who strengthens me!"

We need to make up our minds to abide in Him and then center on the fact that when we abide in Him, He abides with us and enables us to bear much fruit.

Power in Prayer

What kind of fruit will we bear? Prayer fruit, for one thing. Jesus promised that if we would maintain a vital union with Him and keep His Word alive in us, our prayers would produce results.

Some people try to minimize prayer failures by saying, "Well, that's just how God is. Sometimes He answers us by saying yes and sometimes He answers by saying no." That may sound very nice and "spiritual," but it contradicts the words of Jesus. He said, "If ye abide in me, and my words abide in you, ye shall ask what ye will, and it shall be done unto you."

Jesus wasn't speaking idly. He meant every word of that promise. He intends for us to receive everything we ask for in prayer. But He prefaced that promise with two "ifs." You should always watch for the "ifs" in the Bible! He said, "If you abide in Me, and if My words abide in you."

If you are maintaining a living connection with Him and His Word is abundant in you and speaking to your heart, when you pray, you'll see results. You'll have the forces of life and faith coming out of you so that you will reach out into this natural world and change circumstances when you pray. Your faith will be strong.

Those who don't maintain that living connection with God won't experience that kind of prayer power. Spiritually they'll wither and become like those dead branches that men gather and cast into the fire. Instead of triumphing over the devil and the foul circumstances he brings them, the devil will triumph over them.

Christians who don't stay connected to God on a continual basis—who don't talk to Him and give attention to His Word—become a prey for Satan and his evil works. When he comes into their lives to kill, steal and destroy, they won't have the strength to overcome him. Even though according to the Word they are overcomers, in a time of trouble, they'll find themselves too weak to use the authority God has given them.

They may not be bad people. They may not deserve the destruction the devil brings them, but the devil doesn't give people what they deserve; he does whatever he can get away with. And when he finds a Christian who has broken his connection with God, he knows he can get away with plenty!

I heard one preacher say it this way: "If you give the devil a ride, pretty soon he'll be wanting to drive." That's the way the devil is. If you don't tell him what to do, he'll tell you what to do. If you let him get away with one thing, he'll try two.

So, you just can't afford to give him an inch. "Neither give place to the devil" (Ephesians 4:27). You can't afford to miss your time with the Lord, because you need to be able at any moment to exercise the spiritual power that pushes the devil out of your way.

The Fruit of the Spirit

In addition to bearing prayer fruit, abiding in Jesus also enables us to bear all the fruit of the spirit. You can find them listed in Galatians 5:22–23. I especially like *The Amplified Bible* translation of those verses. It says:

> *The fruit of the [Holy] Spirit [the work which His presence within accomplishes] is love, joy (gladness), peace, patience (an even temper, forbearance), kindness, goodness (benevolence), faithfulness, gentleness (meekness, humility), self-control (self-restraint...).*

All those fruit were put within you the moment you were born again. They will forever be a part of your reborn spirit because it is made in the image of God. He put His own divine nature inside you, and each fruit of the spirit is characteristic of His nature.

But even though they are inside you, no matter how hard you work at it, you'll never be able to consistently manifest that fruit in your life unless you are abiding in Jesus, spending time daily in prayer and in the Word. Think about the illustration He gave of the vine and the branches, and you can easily see why that is.

The branch of an apple tree doesn't bear apples because it struggles and strives. It bears apples because it's united to the trunk of the tree, and the life within that tree flowing through the branch just naturally brings forth apples.

In the same way, when you're in union and communion with Jesus—the Vine—His divine life flows through you and produces spiritual fruit. Jesus is your Life Force! Your daily fellowship with Him determines your spiritual results.

Of course, He won't grow the fruit for you any more than the apple tree will take up the responsibility of the branch and grow apples straight from the trunk of the tree. He simply provides you with the power and the life. Then you must do your part by choosing to yield to that life. By an act of your will, you let that which Jesus has put on the inside of you manifest itself on the outside.

For example, when someone says something ugly to you, you have to make a decision. Will you yield to the irritation of your flesh and say something ugly in return? Or will you yield to your spirit and respond in love?

The answer to those questions will be determined by two factors: The first, of course, is the choice you make; the second is the condition of your heart. If you have been daily abiding in fellowship with the Lord, then your heart will be strong and full of the spiritual energy necessary to overrule the flesh and let the love flow.

If you have been neglecting your time with God, however, spending more time in front of the television than in the Word, you may find yourself too weak to obey the direction of the Holy Spirit. Although your heart's desire is to act lovingly, your flesh will win the struggle with your undernourished spirit and lash out in anger toward the one who wronged you.

Rules Have No Power

Later, no doubt, you would be sorry for your action and would probably resolve not to act again in such an ungodly way. You might even start to set up rules for yourself in order to curb your behavior.

Will such rules work? No, because if you aren't abiding in Jesus, you won't have the spiritual strength to keep them. And even if you did, you would be making the same mistake the Christians in Galatia made.

The Galatians lost their hold on the grace of God. They stopped living by faith and started once again to live by Old Testament law. Instead of walking out their salvation through a vital union with God, they were trying to walk it with their own natural strength and abilities.

The Apostle Paul wrote them and said:

O foolish Galatians, who hath bewitched you, that ye should not obey the truth, before whose eyes Jesus Christ hath been evidently set forth, crucified among you? This only would I learn of you, Received ye the Spirit by the works of the law, or by the hearing of faith? Are ye so foolish? having begun in the Spirit, are ye now made perfect by the flesh? (Galatians 3:1–3)

There is nothing unique about the Galatians. Many modern-day believers are unwittingly following in their footsteps. As a result, we continually see two methods of living the Christian life demonstrated in the Church today. As Bible scholar Kenneth Wuest wrote:

> *One (of these methods) is...dependence upon the Holy Spirit for the supply of both the desire and the power to do the will of God. This method results in a life [in which] the fruit of the spirit [is] evident. The other method is that of putting one's self under law, and by self effort attempting to obey that law. This results in a defeated life.*[1]

Many sincere believers find themselves in this position because they either don't know how to hear from the Holy Spirit and make the correct adjustments and yield to His strength, or they don't give God their attention so that they stay full of the Spirit of God. They are not availing themselves of the God-appointed method of living the Christian life, which is union and living communion with God.

God never intended for the Christian life to be lived by a set of rules. He doesn't want it to be lived by law. He wants us to have a heart for Him.

Do you know what living by the law is? It's doing something not because you want to do it, but because you're supposed to do it. It's attending church because it's the "right" thing to do, when you would really rather be somewhere else.

That kind of living doesn't please God, even though it looks good to the eyes of men. If you think about it, you can understand why. How would you feel if someone did something nice for you and then you found out that they didn't really want to do it? You wouldn't like it very much, would you?

How would you feel if someone came to visit you and you knew they really didn't come because they liked you and wanted to see you; they came because they felt obligated to come? You would probably prefer they had just saved themselves the effort and stayed home.

Likewise, the Father desires His children to fellowship with Him because they love Him and want Him in their lives.

The Christian Life Is Simple

God wants us to do the right thing. He wants us to go to church and to act in love. He wants us to serve Him. But He wants us to do those things because we have a heartfelt desire to do them. And that takes us right back to abiding in Him.

It's only by spending time with God that we develop those kinds of desires. And the more we fellowship with Him, the more they grow.

I know it probably amazes worldly people—and even some religious people—when they see thousands of people come to our conventions and spend an entire week, all day and all evening, listening to the Word of God. Many of the believers who come use their vacation time to be able to attend.

No doubt their co-workers say, "What?! You're planning to spend your entire vacation at church?" They think someone who would do that must either be crazy or have a tremendous amount of religious discipline. They can't imagine wanting to spend one day in church, much less a whole week. But the fact is, that's exactly what these believers want to do.

They don't come to hear the Word because they think they have to do it to satisfy some religious requirement. They do it because they would rather be where the Word of God is being preached than anywhere else in the world! They've developed that desire by abiding in Jesus and spending time with Him.

Of course, not everyone who comes to our conventions is like that. There are always some who hear a little about faith, find out that if they'll act on the Word it will bring blessings into their lives, and think, *Well, I'll try that.* So they listen to a tape or two and come to a few meetings and then try to put what they've learned into action, without ever establishing a lifestyle of living communion with God. They try to work faith like a formula. But faith is not a formula. Living and walking every day with the Lord is what makes faith work.

People like that eventually grow tired of trying to remember all the steps and trying to make things work in their own strength, so they quit. "That faith stuff is too hard! It doesn't work," they'll say.

But they're mistaken. The life of faith isn't hard, and it does work. In fact, as Rufus Moseley once wrote, "When one is enough in the spirit, things are done without effort."

Let this truth be written on your heart: *The Christian life is simple when you abide in Jesus through prayer and through the Word. When you don't—it's impossible.*

It doesn't matter if you've been saved and in the ministry for twenty-five years. It doesn't matter if you have great gifts of the Spirit operating in your life. If you stop communing and communicating with God on a daily basis, you'll begin to slip. Even though you know the right things to do, you won't do them.

That's because communion with God can't be stored up. It can't be learned like some dusty old doctrine, and then put away. It has to be maintained on a daily basis. If you want to have a fruitful life, fellowship with God every day. Abide in Him continually, and you will see a tremendous difference in the power and productivity in your life.

CHAPTER 5

It's More Than Possible— It's Inevitable!

Abiding in the Vine doesn't just make it possible for you to bear spiritual fruit—it ensures that you will! That's right! If you abide and maintain a living connection with God, fruit is inevitable.

Jesus told us so in John 15:5. He said, "I am the vine, ye are the branches: He that abideth in me, and I in him, the same bringeth forth much fruit...." Notice Jesus didn't say, "If you abide in Me, you *might* bring forth fruit," or "If you abide in Me, you will *probably* bring forth fruit." He said, *"You will!"* The fruit of the spirit always flourish when we maintain living fellowship with the Lord.

That's good news, because the fruit of the spirit are more than just nice characteristics. They are powerful, supernatural forces. And if we want to live on this earth in victory, we must have those forces at work in our lives.

I won't take the time in this chapter to examine in depth all the fruit of the spirit; that would take a book in itself. I do, however, want to briefly look at some of them, so you can see how they grow when we spend time abiding in Jesus.

Take joy, for example. Jesus mentioned it specifically when He talked to His disciples about abiding. He said, "These things have I spoken unto you, that my joy might remain in you, and that your joy might be full" (John 15:11).

What would keep their joy full? Abiding in the Vine—staying in contact and in communion with Him.

The Apostle Paul echoed this truth in Colossians 2:7 when he said, "See that you go on growing in the Lord, and become strong and vigorous in the truth you were taught. Let your lives overflow with joy..." (TLB).

Joy is an extremely important spiritual force. You must have it to live as an overcomer in this world because "the joy of the LORD is your strength" (Nehemiah 8:10), and without strength you can't win the battles of life.

The only place you can obtain joy is from God. Some people don't realize that. They think you can receive joy from the world. They're wrong. Natural things don't bring joy. They might bring you a moment of happiness. But even that will be fleeting at best, because the same world that makes you happy one moment will turn on you and make you sad the next.

God is the only true generator of joy. It's one of His primary characteristics. If you're depressed, just start hanging around Him. The Bible says that "in [His] presence is fulness of joy" (Psalm 16:11).

It may surprise you to hear this, but heaven is not a sad place. People are laughing there. They're singing and dancing and having a wonderful time because they're dwelling in the presence of God. They're full of the joy of the Lord.

But, praise God, we don't have to wait till we die to join in the fun! We can come into the presence of God while we're still in these natural bodies, because we are born of God and our citizenship is in heaven.

It's true! When you maintain a living connection with God, when you keep His Word abiding in your heart and fellowship with Him continually, you can have "days of heaven upon the earth" (Deuteronomy 11:21). Does that mean you won't have any problems? No. It simply means that when your circumstances aren't good, you don't have to feel miserable about it. You can just maintain your union with the Lord and let His joy start bubbling up within you.

That joy will give you the strength you need to keep on walking in faith until the problem is solved.

Faithfulness, Love, Patience . . . and More

"But, Gloria," you may say, "I'm not just running short on joy these days; I'm also having trouble walking consistently in faith. I'm strong in the Lord one day and weak the next."

No problem! Faithfulness is another fruit of the spirit that flourishes when you maintain a living connection with God. So if you're lacking in faithfulness, all you need to do is start spending time each day fellowshiping with the Lord in His Word.

Faithfulness could be defined as being full of faith; believing; strong or firm in one's faith, firmly adhering to duty; of true fidelity, loyal, true to allegiance; constant in the performances of duties or services. To be faithful is to be trustworthy and dependable. If you want a perfect picture of faithfulness, look at God Himself, for He is faithful! (See 1 Corinthians 1:9.)

Actually, in the New Testament, the Greek word for *faithfulness* can also be translated faith. So, faith and faithfulness are very closely related.

You might say it this way. Faith is faithfulness to God's Word. Faith is being faithful to believe what God says, even when circumstances, obstacles or people seem to contradict His Word.

Staying in constant communion with God will cause you to grow in faithfulness to Him. It will strengthen you in your walk of faith so that you can reach out and receive the blessings of God—blessings such as healing, prosperity and protection. Proverbs 28:20 promises, "A faithful man shall abound with blessings...."

You see, everything we need in this life Jesus has already bought with His blood. As Galatians 3:13–14 says:

> *Christ hath redeemed us from the curse of the law, being made a curse for us: for it is written, Cursed is every one that hangeth on a tree: That the blessing of Abraham might come on the Gentiles through Jesus Christ; that we might receive the promise of the Spirit through faith.*

If you'll read Deuteronomy 28, you'll see that every good thing imaginable is included in God's blessing and every bad thing imaginable is included in the curse. So we're set up in style! God has already provided everything we could ever need. We don't have to talk Him into giving us these things. They're already ours. The blessing has "come on" us!

All we have to do is put ourselves in a position to receive. And the primary key to receiving is faithfulness. We must be faithful to believe and faithful to act on the Word of God.

Of course, before you can even begin to believe God's Word,

you must know what He has said, for "faith cometh by hearing, and hearing by the word of God" (Romans 10:17). But to be faithful to the Word, you must do more than casually read it now and then. You must hear it, believe it and act on it consistently. And to do that, you must have confidence in the One who spoke that Word. You must have confidence in God.

Such confidence is developed by spending time with Him. Just as you grow to trust another person by getting to know him better—by listening to him speak and deepening your relationship with him—so it is with God. The more time you spend with Him, the better you will know Him—and the better you know Him, the greater your confidence in Him will be.

That confidence will enable you to faithfully take God at His Word. You won't sit around wondering if He will do what He said. You won't believe Him one day and doubt Him the next. You'll be able to consistently believe and act like His Word is true, even when circumstances indicate that it isn't.

When you're in constant fellowship and communion with God every day, you will be able to look beyond the circumstances that are staring you in the face and screaming at you, *You'll go bankrupt!* or *You'll die young!* You'll have the strength of character to see past those circumstances and focus instead on the power and love of God and His ability to bring you through in victory.

In his book on the fruit of the spirit, Donald Gee wonderfully illustrates how living fellowship with the Spirit of God brings forth faithfulness in our lives.

Our human natures in all their unreliability [are like]... the loose powder of cement. But when water is mixed with the cement it turns into concrete hard as a rock. So the living water of God's Holy Spirit can turn our lack of stead-fastness into magnificent faithfulness, and convert many an impulsive "Simon" into a devoted "Peter."[2]

That in itself is reason enough to spend time everyday in the Word and in prayer. But there are more reasons still!

Daily fellowship with God will not just cause joy and faithfulness to flourish, it will cause all the rest of the fruit of the spirit to grow in your life. It will empower you to walk in love, and that is vital because love never fails! (We'll talk more about love later.)

It will enable you to live in peace. It will also strengthen your ability to be patient. Patience is a powerful force that undergirds your faith and keeps you from quitting when tests and trials come. When patience is operating in your life, instead of succumbing to the pressure of circumstances, you will be able to keep believing God until circumstances change.

Freedom from Sin

Self-control is another powerful fruit of the Spirit. Constant communion and fellowship with God will give you the power to become temperate in every area of your life and to have self-control. You will be able to keep your body under subjection to your spirit so that your body will do what it's supposed to do. Self-control will enable you to conquer strongholds of sin that for years may have been conquering you!

Some people expect to be free of such strongholds the moment they are born again. But, in most cases, acquiring that freedom is a process that takes place over time. That's because the new birth takes place in our spirit. It makes us new on the inside, but on the outside we have the same old bodies, usually with the same old habits.

The challenge of the Christian life lies in bringing the salvation that's on the inside through to the outside. Our job is to follow the instructions in Ephesians 4:22–24:

> *Strip yourselves of your former nature [put off and discard your old unrenewed self] which characterized your previous manner of life and becomes corrupt through lusts and desires... And be constantly renewed in the spirit of your mind [having a fresh mental and spiritual attitude], And put on the new nature (the regenerate self) created in God's image, [Godlike] in true righteousness and holiness.* (AMP)

We must learn, as the Apostle Paul said, to keep our bodies under and bring them into subjection to our reborn spirit. (See 1 Corinthians 9:27.) We must strengthen our spirit so it can take authority over the body and tell it what to do.

Fellowshiping with God—in prayer and His written Word— helps us do that. When we spend time meditating on the Word, it works like spiritual food, strengthening the inner man, so we can rise up on the inside and take dominion over those fleshly sins and weaknesses that hinder us. It purifies us of ungodly thoughts, attitudes and behaviors and keeps us abiding in Him. It keeps our thinking straight.

As Jesus said in John 15:2–3:

Every branch in me that beareth not fruit he taketh away:
and every branch that beareth fruit, he purgeth it, that it
may bring forth more fruit. Now ye are clean through the
word which I have spoken unto you.

Staying in contact with God and in communion with Him through His Word will cleanse you from sin in two ways: first, by feeding your spirit; and second, by starving your flesh.

Just as the power and fruit of the spirit wither when you lose your communion with God, the power of sin withers when you maintain communion with Him. That is the principle of abiding in the Vine.

As I said before, to *wither* is to shrivel; to lose or cause to lose energy, force or freshness. When you maintain your union with God, sin withers in your life. It has no force to feed it, so it shrivels up and dies.

If you've been struggling with sin, cut off the devil's influence in your life by turning your attention away from worldly things and to the Lord. Spend time every day fellowshiping with God in His Word. Spend time daily praying and worshiping in God's presence.

Do what Colossians 3:2 says and "Set your affection on things above, not on things on the earth." When you do that, sin will lose its appeal and its power. You won't even be tempted to do some of the things you used to do. And those things you are tempted to do, you'll have the power to resist. You'll have the spiritual strength flowing through you to follow the instructions in Romans 6:11–14:

Even so consider yourselves also dead to sin and your relation to it broken, but alive to God [living in unbroken fellowship with Him] in Christ Jesus. Let not sin therefore rule as king in your mortal... bodies, to make you yield to its cravings and be subject to its lusts and evil passions. Do not continue offering or yielding your bodily members [and faculties] to sin as instruments (tools) of wickedness. But offer and yield yourselves to God as though you have been raised from the dead to [perpetual] life, and your bodily members [and faculties] to God, presenting them as implements of righteousness. For sin shall not [any longer] exert dominion over you... (AMP)

Fellowshiping with God on a continual basis and maintaining a living connection with Him will enable you to keep your body under control so that sin doesn't obtain a foothold in your life.

One of the best examples of that truth is one Ken often gives from his own life. He began smoking at a very young age. As he tells it, he thoroughly enjoyed smoking. But when he made Jesus the Lord of his life, he began wanting to break that habit.

The problem was that he couldn't. He tried and tried. He would decide to quit while he was driving down the highway and would throw his cigarettes out the window. A few minutes later, he'd turn the car around to go back and look for them. He was miserable about it.

Then he went down to Houston and spent three weeks in a meeting where the living Word of God was being preached. He spent all day every day listening to that Word and fellowshiping with the Lord.

Do you know what happened? He forgot about those cigarettes! When the meeting was over, he sat down in his car to drive home and realized the cigarettes he'd left tucked above the visor were still there. He hadn't smoked for days. That tobacco habit had withered and died. It no longer had the strength to control him. He was free!

Wouldn't you like to experience that kind of freedom? Wouldn't it be wonderful if you were so abounding in the fruit of the spirit that the words that best described you were the ones found in Galatians 5:22–23?

Love, joy, peace, patience, kindness, goodness, faithfulness, gentleness and self-control—what a heavenly kind of life those forces bring you. Such a life can actually be yours! The life of God flowing through you has the power to produce that fruit in you.

Looking at where you are right now you may wonder, *Is it really possible?*

It's more than possible—it's promised. And if you abide in Jesus, it's inevitable.

CHAPTER 6

Pleasing the Father

There is nothing that pleases the Father more than abiding in the Vine, because as you experience a relationship with Jesus by abiding in Him, you will desire to have more of God. Right now I'm hungrier for God than I have ever been in my life. *I'm hungry to know Him better.* I'm hungry for a greater manifestation of His presence. I'm hungry for Jesus to be fully formed in me.

I'm not alone in that desire. Far from it. Everywhere I go, I see believers who are desiring more of God. I meet Christians whose hearts are crying out to be changed and filled with greater degrees of the glory of God.

A sense of urgency has been implanted in our spirit by the Spirit of God because the end of this age is very near. Time is running out, and God is fulfilling His plan in us. He is preparing for Himself a glorious Church without spot or wrinkle. He is raising up a people who will walk in the things He has prepared for them.

God is bringing forth a multitude of believers who will fulfill the divine destiny prepared for them since the beginning of time. That destiny is defined clearly in Romans 8:29:

*For those whom [God] foreknew [of whom He was aware
and loved beforehand] He also destined from the beginning
[foreordaining them] to be molded into the image of His Son
[and share inwardly His likeness], that He might become the
first-born among many brethren.* (AMP)

Our destiny as believers is to grow up in Jesus. It's to be fully
conformed to His image, which was placed within us the moment
we were born again.

It's a staggering thought that you and I could ever truly be
transformed into that divine image. It seems almost impossible
that we could be like Jesus. But God says we can be. In fact, the
Bible says He has equipped us with everything necessary so that
we might continue growing and developing:

*Until we all attain oneness in the faith and in the compre-
hension of the [full and accurate] knowledge of the Son of
God, that [we might arrive] at really mature manhood (the
completeness of personality which is nothing less than the
standard height of Christ's own perfection), the measure of
the stature of the fullness of the Christ and the completeness
found in Him.* (Ephesians 4:13, AMP)

If anyone other than the Spirit of God had written that, I wouldn't
be able to believe it. But the Spirit of God *did* write it! So, as amazing as it seems, we must simply believe that He has the ability to so
completely conform us to Jesus that we "... become a body wholly
filled and flooded with God Himself!" (Ephesians 3:19, AMP).

We Must Do Our Part

Not only is God able to conform us to the image of Jesus, it is His will for us. It is His end-time plan. But whether or not that divine will comes to pass in our own individual lives is up to us. If we want to be a part of God's plan, we must do our part of God's plan.

That's how it has always been. In Genesis 18:19, God said of Abraham: "For I know him, that he will command his children and his household after him, and they shall keep the way of the Lord, to do justice and judgment; that the Lord may bring upon Abraham that which he hath spoken of him."

Abraham's part was to cooperate with the Lord. If Abraham didn't do that, if he didn't obey what God told him to do, God couldn't fulfill His promise to make Abraham a father of many nations, even though that was His will.

The same is true for us today. It is God's will that we be conformed to the image of Jesus. It is His will to manifest Himself in our lives just as He manifested Himself through Jesus' life. But He will not do it until we do our part.

Our part is simply this: *to walk pleasing before Him—to think His thoughts and speak His words. In other words, we are to walk in His ways.*

If we want to fulfill our divine destiny and enjoy the fullness of the power of God in our lives, we must make a decision and a determination to stop living to please ourselves and start living every moment to please the Father. We must walk out the prayer the Apostle Paul prayed for the Colossians:

*That ye might be filled with the knowledge of [God's]
will in all wisdom and spiritual understanding; that ye
might walk worthy of the Lord unto all pleasing, being fruitful in every good work, and increasing in the knowledge of
God; strengthened with all might, according to his glorious
power...* (Colossians 1:9–11)

Notice that this passage connects pleasing the Lord with the
manifestation of God's glorious power. It says they come together.

The life of Jesus was proof. He said, "He that sent me is with
me: the Father hath not left me alone; for I do always those things
that please him" (John 8:29).

We talk a lot about the fact that God will never leave us nor forsake us. And it's true, He is always with us. But we have to admit,
His power is not always in manifestation.

In Jesus' life, however, God's power was constantly in manifestation. Every moment Jesus walked in the measureless, manifest
power and presence of God because He always did those things
that pleased the Father.

*I am able to do nothing from Myself [independently, of
My own accord—but as I am taught by God and as I get His
orders]. Even as I hear, I judge [I decide as I am bidden to
decide. As the voice comes to Me, so I give a decision], and
My judgment is right (just, righteous), because I do not seek
or consult My own will [I have no desire to do what is pleasing to Myself, My own aim, My own purpose] but only the will
and pleasure of the Father Who sent Me.* (John 5:30, AMP)

> *And He Who sent Me is ever with Me; My Father has not left Me alone, for I always do what pleases Him.* (John 8:29, AMP)

God was able to say of Him, "Thou art my beloved Son, in whom I am well pleased" (Mark 1:11).

Light . . . Not Twilight!

There's no reason why we as believers can't please God as much as Jesus did. We have a reborn spirit made in His image. We've been given His righteousness. We've been filled with the same Holy Spirit. We have all the capacity that Jesus had in the earth to be just like Him and to do the works He did *because He lives in us.* The scripture says ". . . Christ in you, the hope of glory" (Colossians 1:27).

He was dedicated. He was totally sold out to God. He was without sin. The Bible tells us that many times He ministered to the multitudes all day and then prayed all night, yet Jesus had a flesh and blood body just like yours and mine. He enjoyed a good night's sleep just as much as we do. So there was an element of crucifying the flesh involved in giving up that sleep and doing what pleased God. In other words, He had to say *no* to His flesh, and *yes* to the Father.

"Well, Gloria, I know Jesus did that, but God doesn't expect that kind of self-sacrifice from us."

Yes, He does. First Peter 4:1–3 says:

So, since Christ suffered in the flesh for us, for you, arm yourselves with the same thought and purpose [patiently to suffer rather than fail to please God]. For whoever has suffered in the flesh [having the mind of Christ] is done with [intentional] sin—has stopped pleasing himself and the world, and pleases God. So that he can no longer spend the rest of his natural life living by [his] human appetites and desires, but [he lives] for what God wills. For the time that is past already suffices for doing what the Gentiles like to do... (AMP)

It's time for the Church to stop living like Gentiles (heathen) do! It's time for the Church to live like God says, regardless of what the world around us is doing.

It doesn't matter how dark this world becomes, we are to be light in this world. Not the *twilight* of the world but *light!*

We need to fight against compromise by arming ourselves with the commitment to *suffer in the flesh* rather than fail to please God. To suffer in the flesh doesn't mean to bear sickness and poverty without complaining. Jesus already bore sickness and poverty for us, along with every other curse of the broken law, so that we can be free from those things. We are expected to resist that curse in Jesus' Name.

Suffering in the flesh is making your flesh do something it doesn't want to do. It's dedicating yourself to do what's pleasing to God even when it causes your flesh discomfort.

When you're ready to do that, you'll go beyond just "not sinning" and into a life that's pleasing to God. You'll be ready to lay down things you enjoy, things that aren't necessarily bad in themselves, yet which are hindering your walk with God.

If you want to walk in the best God has for you, those are the kinds of sacrifices you must make, for Jesus said:

> *He who does not take up his cross and follow Me [cleave steadfastly to Me, conforming wholly to My example in living and, if need be, in dying also] is not worthy of Me. Whoever finds his [lower] life will lose [the higher life], and whosoever loses his [lower] life on My account will find [the higher life].* (Matthew 10:38–39, AMP)

If you could see what God has for you in the higher life, you would immediately let go of the mundane things of the world. But you're not going to be able to see it and *then* make your decision.

You have to step into that higher life by faith. You have to lay down your life because the Word says to do it. Then and only then will you discover the wonders that are waiting on the other side of your obedience.

I'm sure Enoch didn't know what the higher life held for him. He probably had no idea that he'd be the first man ever raptured. Hebrews 11:5 says, "By faith Enoch was translated that he should not see death...for before his translation he had this testimony, that *he pleased God*."

Righteousness and Holiness: Two Different Things

How do you develop the spiritual strength to do the things that please the Father, rather than the things that please yourself? *First and foremost, by spending time in the Word and in prayer.* When the power of God was being displayed through the early apostles in great signs and wonders, that's what they were doing. They were giving themselves "continually to prayer, and to the ministry of the word" (Acts 6:4).

Romans 8:5 says it this way: "For they that are after the flesh do mind the things of the flesh; but they that are after the Spirit the things of the Spirit." That is the matter in a nutshell. If you want to grow physically and build big muscles, you have to spend time lifting weights and doing physical things to build those muscles. If you want to grow spiritually, you will have to spend time doing spiritual things.

As you spend time fellowshiping with God in His Word, the Holy Spirit, by the power of that Word, will separate you not only from sin, but also from the unnecessary things of life. He will impart to you the spiritual might and grace you need to obey Ephesians 4:22–24:

> *Strip yourselves of your former nature... and be constantly renewed in the spirit of your mind... and put on the new nature (the regenerate self) created in God's image, [Godlike] in true righteousness and holiness.* (AMP)

Righteousness and holiness are to be put on. But true righteousness and true holiness come from the inside to the outside.

Verse 24 tells us that righteousness and holiness are two different things. Righteousness is the right standing with God you gained when you were born again. The only thing you did to be made righteous was to make Jesus Christ the Lord of your life.

Holiness, however, is another matter. You are not *made* holy. Holiness is the result of your choices. It's what you do with your time and your actions. It's your conduct. It comes when you make a decision of your will to live according to the precepts of the Lord. In short, holiness is doing those things that please the Father.

To be holy is to be "sanctified, and meet for the master's use" (2 Timothy 2:21). *Sanctified* means "set apart." Set apart from what? From the world! God wants us to be so caught up in spiritual things that we lose interest in carnal activities and pursue Him with all our hearts.

He doesn't want us simply to obey a set of rules because it's the "right thing to do." That's law instead of spirit. God wants us to live holy lives because we have a heartfelt desire to please Him. When we spend time with the Lord, we *want* to do the things that please Him. Our desire is for spiritual things, not the things of the flesh. It shouldn't be a "head thing" but a "heart thing." Time *with* Him separates us *to* Him. Spending time with God will bring union and agreement. He wants us to love Him so much that we are wholly dedicated to Him!

We should not consider such holiness as something out of the ordinary. God expects us all to live holy. He says, "Be ye holy; for I am holy" (1 Peter 1:16).

Certainly such a life will require us to make some sacrifices. It will cause us to suffer in the flesh at times. But it will be worth it. For "the sufferings of this present time are not worthy to be compared with the glory which shall be revealed in us" (Romans 8:18).

When you see the power and glory of God start to flow in greater measure through you, you won't regret that you made those sacrifices. You'll be glad! When you lay hands on a crippled person and see him raised instantly out of a wheelchair, you'll be glad you turned down natural, carnal things for supernatural spiritual things. You'll be glad you gave up those hours of sleep so you could spend extra time in the Word and in prayer. Walking in the spirit is a bargain at any price!

When you speak in the Name of Jesus to someone in bondage, and the devil instantly flees and they go free, you won't be wishing you'd spent more time pleasing yourself. You'll be thanking God you chose to please Him instead.

You may think I'm being overly dramatic, but I'm not. Those things are going to happen—not just at the hands of famous preachers and full-time ministers, but at the hands of everyday believers. We've already started to see it. But we're just on the edge of what's coming. We haven't seen anything yet!

The prophets of God are telling us that we are about to see the greatest outpouring of God's power this earth has ever known.

Glory to God, we are about to see multitudes of Christians put aside the distractions of this age and rise up in the strength of God Himself! We are about to see believers conformed to the image of Jesus on the outside as well as the inside! We are about to see the Church that God has always dreamed of—a Church holy and without blemish!

Determine in your heart to be a vital part of this great move of God. Make up your mind that you won't be sidelined by doing petty things that please yourself. Dedicate yourself to live wholly pleasing to the Father—and get ready for a life of power!

CHAPTER 7

A Living Sacrifice

I beseech you therefore, brethren, by the mercies of God, that ye present your bodies a living sacrifice, holy, acceptable unto God, which is your reasonable service. And be not conformed to this world: but be ye transformed by the renewing of your mind, that ye may prove what is that good, and acceptable, and perfect, will of God. (Romans 12:1–2)

We are not to be conformed to this world, but we are to present our bodies a living, holy sacrifice, not conformed to the world but transformed by the renewing of our minds to the will of God.

When we lay aside the things of the world and give our attention to spiritual things, we walk in the glory that God wants to reveal in us. Therefore, it's very important that we are willing to change our attitudes and our priorities to please Him. We are to make our lives living sacrifices to Him, holy unto the Lord.

The manifestation of God's power is directly related to holiness in the Body of Christ. God does not manifest Himself through those who are disobedient and have sin in their lives. So the Holy Spirit works in us to bring our consciousness, or awareness, into agreement with Him. At the same time, Satan works without to keep us bound to this world. Therefore, we must defeat the enemy's wiles and choose to walk in the spirit, being led by the Holy Spirit and by God's Word, if we are to be vessels of honor and power.

Second Timothy 2:21 says that if a man will purge himself of iniquity, he will be a vessel of honor, prepared for every good work. Notice who does the purging. The man himself!

And what agreement hath the temple of God with idols? for ye are the temple of the living God; as God hath said, I will dwell in them, and walk in them; and I will be their God, and they shall be my people.... Having therefore these promises, dearly beloved, let us cleanse ourselves from all filthiness of the flesh and spirit, perfecting holiness in the fear of God. (2 Corinthians 6:16, 7:1)

Do Not Be Drawn Away

Let no man say when he is tempted, I am tempted of God: for God cannot be tempted with evil, neither tempteth he any man: But every man is tempted, when he is drawn away of his own lust, and enticed. Then when lust hath conceived, it bringeth forth sin: and sin, when it is finished, bringeth forth death. (James 1:13–15)

This scripture says we are tempted when we are drawn away. Drawn away from what? From God. As new creatures in Christ Jesus, our inner man wants to do the will of God. Our hearts want to please Him and to do what is right in His sight. We, however, have to contend with the temptations of the flesh. We still live in a natural body that must be dominated by the spirit—the new creature on the inside.

The word most often associated with *flesh* is the term "lust." In our thinking it is connected with sex or immorality. But in the Greek, the word simply means "strong desire." The lust of the flesh is the strong desire to follow after the ways of the world, rather than after God. For instance, a lust for money can pull you away from God.

It is acceptable to have a desire for success, or to obtain an education or career, or even to be recognized in your profession. These "wants" are permissible if they are kept in perspective—behind God. But we must always be watchful that these things do not draw us away from God, and that we follow God's will for our lives. Our strong desire must be for God.

The Father wants us to be successful. On the other hand, Jesus said, "What does it profit a man if he gains the whole world and loses his own soul?"

We do not want to be drawn away from God through fleshly desires. We can walk and function in this world without being subjected to it. (See John 17:16.) As believers, we are already citizens of the kingdom of heaven. We are not of this world.

Be Sensitive to the Holy Spirit

In the past we were debtors to the flesh. But now God is calling us to set our affection on things above. He wants us to give our attention to the things of the spirit so we can dominate the world around us with the love and power of God. God has patiently waited for the Church. It is time for His power and glory to be manifest as it has never been before.

The Lord told Kenneth that there are three things we would have to do to move in the flow of the Holy Spirit: 1) We must purge ourselves of sin; 2) we must intercede; and 3) we must prepare for criticism.

> But if the Spirit of him that raised up Jesus from the dead dwell in you, he that raised up Christ from the dead shall also quicken your mortal bodies by his Spirit that dwelleth in you. Therefore, brethren, we are debtors, not to the flesh, to live after the flesh. For if ye live after the flesh, ye shall die: but if ye through the Spirit do mortify the deeds of the body, ye shall live. For as many as are led by the Spirit of God, they are the sons of God. (Romans 8:11–14)

In the Old Testament God's children were very careful about the dwelling place of the Spirit of God. We must consider who is living in us! We are walking temples of the Holy Ghost! "I will be a Father to them," God said. "I will dwell in them and walk in them."

The same Spirit that raised Jesus from the dead will raise you from the bondage of a mortal body. He quickened the mortal flesh of Jesus and He will quicken our mortal flesh by His Spirit. But we have to give Him a place. You must be sensitive to Him and be ever conscious of His presence.

The Holy Spirit is not a dictator. He will move only when you yield to Him. He is our strengthener. He is the One called alongside to help. He cannot assist us if we will not participate with Him in spiritual action. We must be aware of His presence and cooperate with Him.

Offer Yourself

Romans 12:1–2 talks about crucifying the flesh: "Present your bodies a living sacrifice...." So does Galatians 5:24–25: "And they that are Christ's have crucified the flesh with the affections and lusts. If we live in the Spirit, let us also walk in the Spirit." We are admonished to offer our bodies as living sacrifices. We are to lay aside our own natural desires in order to fulfill God's desires. The Wuest translation says that we are to place our bodies at the disposal of God.[3]

According to the Bible, this is only our reasonable service, although it might seem an unreasonable demand to some. Why is it our reasonable service? Because Jesus gave His body as a living sacrifice for us. We have been bought with a price, and we are to glorify God in our bodies and in our spirits. (See 1 Corinthians 6:19–20.)

The Greek word translated *Lord* means "master" or "owner."[4] Jesus became your new owner the moment you made Him the Lord of your life. Most Christians get born again but will not allow Jesus to be Lord in their lives. They choose to continue to walk in the darkness of this world, when they could walk in the light of God.

"[The Father] has delivered and drawn us to Himself out of the control and the dominion of darkness and has transferred us into the kingdom of the Son of His love" (Colossians 1:13, AMP). We have been transferred into the kingdom of God. We are to place our bodies and our minds at the disposal of God and allow the Holy Spirit to teach us how to live under the dominion of God.

This sacrifice of our body is to be a holy and well-pleasing (acceptable) sacrifice. The Greek word *thusia*, translated sacrifice, denotes "the act of offering." We are to make an offering of our bodies. You are the offering that God desires.

What does God desire of us as a continual offering unto Him? He desires that our bodies not conform to, or be fashioned after, this world, which is patterned after Satan. He wants our bodies at His disposal so He can change them from worldliness to godliness. We are to be transformed by the renewing of our minds. W. E. Vine says the word *renew* means "the adjustment of the moral and spiritual vision and thinking to the mind of God." We are to adjust our thinking to the mind of God. The Holy Spirit teaches us to think like God thinks and to act like God acts. As we do this, the outward expression of our body will begin to match the inward expression of Jesus. We will begin to walk in the good and well-pleasing and perfect will of God.

Offer yourself as a living sacrifice. Lay down your own desires in order to fulfill God's desire. This is not an unreasonable thing for God to ask. This is only your reasonable service, because you have been bought with a precious price. Jesus purchased you with the crucifying of His own flesh, and He shed His blood to redeem you. Jesus became a living sacrifice for you. The least you can do is yield your body to God, for you are not your own.

There is a decision to be made. Are you going to serve your own interests or are you going to serve the Lord Jesus? I believe you are going to decide to offer yourself as a living sacrifice. And when you do, you are going to find that you do not have to fight the war between your flesh and your spirit. Your spirit, controlled by the Holy Spirit, will stop the war! As you choose to obey the Holy Spirit, the law of the Spirit of life that is in Christ Jesus will make you free from the law of sin and death.

Transformed Into His Image

"For whom he did foreknow, he also did predestinate to be conformed to the image of his Son, that he might be the firstborn among many brethren" (Romans 8:29).

You will not be squeezed into the mold of this world. You will look and act just like Jesus! Allow the Holy Spirit to so affect you that you live right here on earth as if you were already in heaven. Heaven has no sin, sickness or lack! You have the Holy Spirit of God on the inside of you. God dwells in you and walks in you. God wants His Body to be vessels of His glory to minister life to the whole world.

For God, who commanded the light to shine out of darkness, hath shined in our hearts, to give the light of the knowledge of the glory of God in the face of Jesus Christ. But we have this treasure in earthen vessels, that the excellency of the power may be of God, and not of us. (2 Corinthians 4:6–7)

God wants the Church to be transformed into the image of Jesus. He wants us to control and dominate the physical world around us. When your body is presented as a living sacrifice, then God will be revealed in you.

Today is the day! Before you do another thing, put this book down and lift your hands to God. Make your body a living sacrifice, holy and acceptable to Him. Ask the Lord to teach you how to walk in the spirit. Believe you receive the wisdom of God. You will never be the same!

CHAPTER 8

Keep the Union

Once we understand the divine power that comes to us as we abide in Jesus, it is easy to see that if we want to live victoriously, we must first and foremost maintain our union and communion with Him. That is without question our most important responsibility.

If we will maintain that union, God will take care of everything else.

Unfortunately, however, many Christians do just the opposite. They become so busy maintaining the other things in their lives that they don't take time to spend with God. They spend their lives maintaining their houses, their lawns, their cars and their jobs. They even find time to maintain their hair and their fingernails. Yet, they neglect the one thing that is vital to their life and well being. They neglect their union with God.

Often they don't even realize it. They think that because they love the Lord and believe His Word, their union with Him is intact. But that's not necessarily so.

To be in union means to be joined together with something or someone. It's the act or instance of joining two or more things into one. Romans 7:4 likens our union with God to marriage. It says we have been married to Him. First Corinthians 6:17 further explains that "the person who is united to the Lord becomes one spirit with Him" (AMP). The word *united* used there (or *joined*, in the *King James Version*) could be replaced with "laminated." It refers to something glued so tightly together that it becomes like one substance.

As we begin to spend time with the Lord, we begin to think like He thinks. We begin to act like He acts. We begin to hear from heaven moment by moment so that we can walk out the perfect will of God for our lives every day.

Our goal is to become so in tune with Him that when He tells us to do something, we hear Him and obey. Our aim is to be so closely joined to Him that the desires of our hearts, the thoughts of our minds, the words of our mouths and our every action become reflections of the One with whom we are united.

That is God's desire too. For if He is to carry out His will in the earth, He must have people who will join themselves with Him in that way. As Rufus Moseley wrote:

> *God has to have branches of the same texture as Himself, the same sap, the same mind, the same spirit, before He can bring forth in fullness what He wants to bring forth....All you have to do to keep the union is to put Him first and keep your mind stayed on Him. In union and in love you will have everything else.[5]*

Perfect Union = Perfect Peace

How do you keep your mind stayed on God? By giving Him your attention. By putting His Word first every day and focusing on it until it is the biggest thing in your life. *The Living Bible* says it this way:

Since you became alive again, so to speak, when Christ arose from the dead, now set your sights on the rich treasures and joys of heaven where he sits beside God in the place of honor and power. Let heaven fill your thoughts... (Colossians 3:1–2)

Spiritually speaking, when you received Jesus as your Lord, you died to this world and became alive to God. So you should have as little desire for this world as a dead person does!

You shouldn't spend your time worrying about worldly concerns. You should spend your time listening to what God has to say. You should keep your mind focused on Him.

Isaiah 26:3 says, "Thou [God] wilt keep him in perfect peace, whose mind is stayed on thee...."

Jesus confirmed that when He said, "Peace I leave with you, my peace I give unto you: not as the world giveth, give I unto you. Let not your heart be troubled, neither let it be afraid" (John 14:27).

The world doesn't have any peace. If you keep your mind on the world and stay in union with it, you won't have any peace either. If you give the majority of your time and attention to worldly matters and secular entertainment, you will be carnally minded, and

the Bible says, "to be carnally minded is death; but to be spiritually minded is life and peace" (Romans 8:6).

In other words, if you think like the world thinks, you will
receive the same results the world receives. Instead of enjoying
the healing power of God, you will suffer with the sicknesses
of the world. Instead of laying hold of heavenly prosperity, the
depression, recession and poverty of the world will lay hold of
you! Instead of being full of good news, you'll be full of bad
news.

Contact with the wrong things and the wrong people will give
you the wrong results, and there are plenty of opportunities to be
in contact with the world's way of thinking. In the United States,
it is possible to watch the news twenty-four hours a day. (It's a ter-
rible curse, but you can do it.) You can turn on the television any
time of the day or night and hear about all the things the devil is
doing.

"Well, Gloria," you say, "we can't stick our heads in the sand.
We have to face the facts."

I'm not suggesting we stick our heads in the sand. I'm suggesting we keep them in the Word!

I am also suggesting that sometimes the news doesn't give us
the facts. I watch the news, but I'm careful about what I believe
from the world's voice. God's voice is my authority.

A few years ago, for example, the media announced that the
United States' economy was in recession. For about a year and a
half, they talked about the recession. News of the recession influenced the elections that year. It influenced everything that happened because the media would constantly broadcast it.

Sometime later a statistical report came out that revealed the recession had actually lasted only a few months. Why, then, had the news media kept on reporting about it? They didn't know it had ended. They were in the dark, so they kept screaming, "Recession! Recession!" even though the recession had been over for more than a year.

Thank heaven, that recession never got off the ground with us. When news of it first came out, the Lord spoke to Ken and said, "Write your Partners and tell them not to join the recession." So we obeyed God and didn't join in. We just let the recession pass us by.

That may sound strange to you, but as citizens of heaven, you and I can do that kind of thing. If we stay in union with God, we don't have to be dependent on this world's economy. We can be connected to heaven's economy, in which there is no recession, depression or inflation. In God's economy there is no shortage or lack of any kind. He is our Shepherd; we shall not want! (See Psalm 23:1.)

If you unite with the world's voice, you will always be in trouble, because the world is always in trouble. But if you'll spend your time listening to what God says and maintain your union with Him—if you'll keep your mind stayed on the Word of God, no matter what the news media says or what the circumstances say, God will deliver you from any trouble. The Lord told my friend Lynne Hammond, "If you'll give Me enough time" (meaning spend enough time with Me), "I can turn anything around for you." He'll meet your needs, not according to the government, not according to what happens in this natural economy, but according to His riches in glory!

The circumstances on this earth don't bother God; He is not

bound by them or limited to them. He can prosper you anytime, anywhere and in any way He wants.

God knows how to prosper people even when they're in slavery! Read the book of Exodus and you can see that for yourself. He brought the Israelites out of slavery in Egypt with silver and gold. The Bible says they plundered the Egyptians. The Egyptians loaded them with treasure and sent them out of the country as rich people!

You're Connected

It doesn't matter how bad things become out there in the world, because you aren't in the world without a Savior! You are "connected to Christ, the Head to which all of us who are his body are joined..." (Colossians 2:19 TLB).

When someone has friends in high places, we sometimes say, "He's connected." Well, if you're maintaining a living connection with God, you're connected! You're connected with the highest ruler and authority in existence. You have a connection with the power above every other power, and you need to maintain an awareness of that connection. You ought to think about it all through the day.

If you'll do that, the faith and power of God will rise up within you to deal with whatever comes your way. Even if it's danger of the worst kind, you'll be ready.

One of our Partners proved that fact in her own life a few years ago. She was traveling on a bus in a major city she was visiting, and some men aboard that bus began to rob the people. They were going from one person to the next, taking money, jewelry and other valuables.

But this lady had been maintaining her union with the Lord. She was strong on the inside and had His power flowing through her. So, when the thieves came to her, something happened. Instead of cowering in fear and handing over her possessions, she looked those men straight in the eye and said, "In the Name of Jesus, you take your hands off me!"

Suddenly it didn't matter that those men were armed. It didn't matter that they were much bigger than she was. Whatever happened in the spirit realm when she spoke those faith words scared those men so badly, they not only left her alone—they ran off that bus!

You may be a 100-pound woman or a 250-pound man. Your physical stature is irrelevant. You become a giant when you're connected to Jesus. You're unbeatable when you're abiding in Him. If you'll maintain a living connection with the Lord, whatever you do, wherever you go, the power of God will be just one Name away—Jesus!

We live in a day when you may need that power at any moment. We are living in the last of the last days, and there is danger all around us. When that danger strikes, we may not have time to go find our Bibles and look up a scripture about protection. We need to have the Word in our hearts. We need to have it dwelling in us so richly that it comes up in us before we even have time to think.

In times of crisis, your mind usually goes blank, and whatever is in your heart comes out. Whatever you have united with flows right out from your innermost being. If you've been fellowshiping with the world, fear will come out. If you've been fellowshiping with God, faith will come out. In good times and bad times, strong union with the Word of God and the Holy Spirit will make all the difference in your life.

CHAPTER 9

Let the Word Abide in You

Although we fellowship with God in a number of ways, the primary avenue through which we have a living connection with Him is through His written Word.

Why do I consider the Word to be the most important? Because the Bible says that "without faith it is impossible to please [God]..." (Hebrews 11:6); therefore, all our dealings with God must be based on faith. And since faith comes by hearing, and hearing by the Word of God (Romans 10:17), the Word provides the foundation for all divine contact.

Take prayer, for example. It is a very important form of fellowship with God. There is no denying that. But faith is essential if you want your prayers to be answered. To have an effective prayer life, you have to know what God has said and believe it. In Mark 11:24 Jesus said, "What things soever ye desire, when ye pray, believe that ye receive them, and ye shall have them."

It is impossible to pray effectively without a knowledge of God's Word, because for the most part, prayers that are not based on the Word are prayers of unbelief. I proved that in my own life.

I prayed at various times throughout my early years, but because I didn't hear the Word until I was a grown woman, most of my prayers were just a rehearsal of the problem.

God already knew the problem! What He needed was for me to open the door of faith, so He could move into my life and solve that problem. But I didn't have any faith. I didn't know to believe I received when I prayed, as it says to do in Mark 11:24.

What happened as a result of those faithless prayers? For the most part, nothing at all.

"But Gloria," you ask, "couldn't you have prayed for faith?"

Yes, I could have, but I wouldn't have received faith that way because faith doesn't come by praying for it; it comes by hearing the Word of God (Romans 10:17). The only way you can obtain faith is to hear the Word preached or spend time in it yourself!

Of course, you can spend a lifetime studying the Word like a textbook just to gain natural knowledge—just to learn facts—and it won't generate faith or do anything else for you spiritually. For the Word to be effective in your life, you have to let it become more than just a book to you. You must treat it as though God is speaking to you personally through its pages. You must let God's Words jump out of your Bible and into your heart, so they can abide and take up residence there.

God's Word can do that because His words are not just tired, dead, ordinary words. They are supernatural words that originated in heaven. As Hebrews 4:12 says:

For the Word that God speaks is alive and full of power [making it active, operative, energizing, and effective]; it is sharper than any two-edged sword, penetrating to the dividing line of the breath of life (soul) and [the immortal] spirit, and of joints and marrow [of the deepest parts of our nature], exposing and sifting and analyzing and judging the very thoughts and purposes of the heart. (AMP)

All God's words have had His life in them from the moment He first spoke them. And even though they have been written for thousands of years, those words are still as powerful and full of life today as they were the day God spoke them. His words are eternal. Jesus said they are spirit and they are life. (See John 6:63.) So when you take words from the Bible and put them in your heart and in your mouth, they bring whatever they promise to pass by His power—supernaturally!

God's Word travels in a circle. It comes down to us from Him like rain from heaven and goes into the soil of our hearts. (See Mark 4.) When we lift those words back up to Him in prayer by faith, the circle is completed and He brings them to pass in our lives.

Isaiah 55:10–11 says it this way:

For as the rain and snow come down from the heavens, and return not there again, but water the earth and make it bring forth and sprout, that it may give seed to the sower and bread to the eater, So shall My word be that goes forth out of My mouth: it shall not return to Me void [without producing any effect, useless], but it shall accomplish that which I please and purpose, and it shall prosper in the thing for which I sent it. (AMP)

Keep the Word Alive in You

Remember though, if you want the Word to produce this kind of powerful result in your life, you can't be content just to "know" it. You must believe it and meditate on it until it abides in you so that you will obey it. We call that "acting on the Word." First John 2:24 says it like this:

As for you, keep in your hearts what you have heard from the beginning. If what you heard from the first dwells and remains in you, then you will dwell in the Son and in the Father [always]. (AMP)

For yourselves, let the teaching which you have heard from the beginning abide within you. If that teaching does abide within you, you also will abide in the Son and in the Father. (WEYMOUTH)

The secret to the abiding life is to put the Word into your heart in abundance until it overflows in faith and the written Word becomes the living Word in your heart and mouth. Give your attention to it just like God instructed Joshua.

Only you be strong and very courageous, that you may do according to all the law which Moses My servant com-manded you. Turn not from it to the right hand or to the left, that you may prosper wherever you go. This Book of the Law shall not depart out of your mouth, but you shall meditate on it day and night, that you may observe and do according to all that is written in it. For then you shall make your way prosperous, and then you shall deal wisely and have good success. (Joshua 1:7–8, AMP)

I realize, of course, that you can't walk around reading your Bible twenty-four hours a day. But if you're committed to abiding in the Word, you will find time to put it into your heart. You can certainly keep the Word abiding in you twenty-four hours a day.

Ken and I first learned to walk by faith back in the late 1960s by listening to tapes by Kenneth E. Hagin. Back then we didn't have the convenient audio resources that are available now. We had to use the big seven-inch reel-to-reel kind.

Every day I'd hurry and finish my housework so that I could sit down and listen to those tapes. I listened to them so many times and took so many notes that I eventually wrote down word for word a great part of those tapes. I still have my notebook today.

In addition, whenever Brother Hagin held a meeting in Tulsa, we found a way to be there. In the short time we lived there, we went to every service. We didn't miss one of them. We had to slip and slide our way over ice-covered streets to attend some of them, but we did it because we were so desperate for the Word!

That desperation paid off too. Before long, things in our lives began to change. Because we started abiding in the Word, the Word started abiding in us. Jesus said, "If ye abide in me, and my words abide in you, ye shall ask what ye will, and it shall be done unto you" (John 15:7).

How do you know if the Word is abiding in you? It begins to

speak to you. If the Word is not talking to you, then it's not alive in your heart and you need to refresh your remembrance of it. Proverbs 6:20–22 says:

My son, keep thy father's commandment, and forsake not the law of thy mother: Bind them continually upon thine heart, and tie them about thy neck. When thou goest, it shall lead thee ... and when thou awakest, it shall talk with thee.

The Word that is abiding in you—that's alive in you—is the Word that talks to you. It's the Word that leads you moment by moment as you go about your day. The abiding Word will come up in your heart unexpectedly, much like the words and notes of a familiar song might waft spontaneously through your mind.

The Word that is in you in abundance is also the Word that you hear coming out of your mouth, for out "of the abundance of the heart [the] mouth speaketh" (Luke 6:45). If you are in a situation where you need a scripture to come out of your mouth and you find yourself speaking doubt and fear instead, that's an indication that the Word you need to overcome that situation is not alive in you.

To conquer the challenges of the devil, you must have the spiritual strength within you that only the engrafted Word can provide. You have to be so established in that Word that it automatically rises up within you at the moment of crisis. You have to be like the "young men" the Apostle John wrote to saying, "Ye are strong, and the word of God abideth in you, and ye have overcome the wicked one" (1 John 2:14).

No Deposit, No Return

If the Word is not abiding in you as it should—if it's not coming up inside you when you need it—the solution is simple: Spend more time in it. Put more of the Word in your heart and more will come out of your mouth!

In some ways your heart is like a bank account. If you want to write faith checks on that account, you must have plenty of Word in there to back them. Jesus said, "A good man out of the good treasure of his heart bringeth forth that which is good..." (Luke 6:45). Or, as Matthew 12:33–35 says in the *New International Version*:

> *Make a tree good and its fruit will be good, or make a tree bad and its fruit will be bad, for a tree is recognized by its fruit. You brood of vipers, how can you who are evil say anything good? For out of the overflow of the heart the mouth speaks. The good man brings good things out of the good stored up in him, and the evil man brings evil things out of the evil stored up in him.*

If you haven't put money in the bank, when you write a check, money cannot be withdrawn from that account. The Word is the same way. If you haven't deposited God's Word about healing in your heart, when you become sick, faith words of healing will not come out of your mouth. If you haven't deposited God's Word about prosperity in your heart, when the devil attacks your finances, you won't have the spiritual funds to fight back.

"But I did deposit God's Word about healing in my heart," you say. "I read healing scriptures every day last year."

You probably deposited a thousand dollars in the bank a few years ago too—but are you living on that money today? Of course not! It's long gone. You cashed checks on it and used it all.

By the same token, in this life you have to walk by faith, so you are continually writing faith checks. The Word you put in your heart becomes strength and produces—if you believe it and keep it. And you're continually drawing on that supply of strength to meet the challenges that come your way. You are always encountering situations that require supernatural help. So, to keep your strength account from running low, you must continually make deposits of the Word. You must keep a fresh deposit of the Word in your heart at all times by feeding on it every day.

Right now you may not be in a position to make huge deposits of money into your natural bank account. But you can make any size deposit you want to make in your heart account—and that's the account that really matters, because it's the one you draw from to change the circumstances in your life. It holds the faith you'll need to cover any bill the devil tries to send your way.

Remember, faith comes by hearing, and hearing by the Word of God (Romans 10:17). Faith goes by saying, and saying the Word of God (Mark 11:23). If you need healing, make a list of healing scriptures to read and say out loud every day.

It's wise to begin making deposits in the area of your greatest need. If your biggest problem is finances, you should set your attention on the Word of God concerning prosperity. You ought to go to the Word and start the power of God working in you, so faith will rise up in your heart and cause you to prosper.

God wants to help you with your needs. He loves you. He wants to ease your distresses and supply your needs in every area. He wants to help you solve your problems—whether those problems are in your pocketbook, your family, your body or any other area of your life.

God is your Father. He feels about you the way other parents feel about children. They want to bless their children. They want to help their children. Well, so does God! His heart is tender toward His children, and He is always looking for opportunities to bless them. When they believe His Word, it gives Him that opportunity. So let Him in! Open the door of faith to Him by spending time in His Word. Meditate on it until that Word becomes bigger inside you than the circumstances that surround you. Set your attention on the Word that gives you an answer to the problem you're facing. Then focus on God's answer until you can look right past the circumstances and into the realm of the spirit. Focus on it until you can see God's Word coming to pass for you! We call that seeing through the eye of faith.

When you do that, you'll find that poverty, lack, sickness and failure of every kind will wither. They will lose the energy to stay in your life, and the provision of God will gain energy and bring you what you need.

Your future is stored up in your heart! By building your faith account, you'll bankrupt the devil in your life. Satan just won't have the resources to keep you down anymore. If he tries to put sickness on you, you can draw from the Word of God about healing and it will give you victory in that area.

But remember, you can't make a withdrawal from an account that doesn't have anything in it. No deposit, no return!

Some people don't understand that. They see someone else having his circumstances turned around by faith and they think, *Well, faith worked for that person, so I'll just pray the same prayer he did and it will work for me too.*

That's not necessarily true. You may know someone who can write a check for a million dollars, but that doesn't mean you can do it. It depends on whether you've put that much money in your bank account.

If you need more faith in your heart to meet the challenges you're facing right now, put more of God's Word in there. Since faith comes by hearing the Word, you can have as much as you want. However much Word you put in your heart and believe enough to act on is how much faith you have to eliminate the problems in your life.

But remember this—no one can make deposits into your heart account but you. Your spouse can't do it for you. Your pastor can't do it for you. Even God can't do it for you. You're the one who has to open your Bible every day. You're the one who has to listen to teaching resources, go to meetings where the Word is being taught and regularly attend a church where the Word is being preached. You're the one who has to open your ears and your heart and receive the living Word!

When the Word Is Abiding in You, You'll Speak in Faith

It is so important to have the Word abiding in you in abundance, because when you come up against a test or a trial, the devil will put tremendous pressure on you to say negative things. You will find yourself strongly tempted to speak the problem instead of the Word. But you can't finish in victory if you do that.

In Mark 11:23, Jesus taught us that "whosoever shall say ... and shall not doubt in his heart, but shall believe that those things which he saith shall come to pass; he shall have whatsoever he saith." The realm of the spirit works according to our words. We have what we say. Our words are the voice of our faith.

The devil knows that. So when our circumstances are bad, he pushes us to say what we have! He wants us to say, "I feel so sick!" instead of "By Jesus' stripes I am healed." He wants us to say, "I'm broke!" instead of "My God meets my needs according to His riches in glory."

Ken and I were in a hotel elevator sometime ago. We stood in that elevator talking for a while but we didn't go anywhere. Then we realized that instead of pushing the button to go to the floor we wanted, we had pushed the button of the floor where we started. That didn't take us anywhere!

As believers, most of us do the same thing with our words. We say what we have instead of saying what we desire. As a result, things just stay the way they are.

Even if we know we should be speaking the Word, when the pressure of adverse circumstances hits us, we won't say what we should unless we're abiding in the Word and the Word is abiding in us. Even if we did say it, faith that comes from the Word would have to empower those words as Jesus taught in order to change things. Believing in your heart comes from hearing and receiving the Word of God as fact. We may even have to double up and give twice as much time and attention to the Word when we're in especially serious situations. I have a friend who had terminal cancer. She gave all her time to the Word of God until cancer had to depart.

There have been times in my life when the Spirit of God instructed me to go on a veritable "Word binge." (That's my term, not His.) Do you know what a binge is? It's doing a whole lot of something. For example, when you go on a food binge, you eat almost anything you can get your hands on. You eat and eat and eat.

That's what I do with the Word when I'm on a Word binge. I don't watch secular television or do anything else that's not absolutely necessary. I spend all my free time reading the Word, listening to teaching resources, reading good Bible-based books or watching faith preachers on television. And I continue doing that as long as the Lord directs. Actually, it would be a wise and powerful way to live all the time. However much time and attention we give God is how much blessing and anointing come back to us.

In times past when God instructed me to attend to the Word with such intensity, it was because there was a test or trial ahead of me that I didn't know was coming. He wanted me to be extra full of the Word, so I'd be strong and ready for it.

So I suggest that you listen to the Lord when He gives you instructions like that. When He says to you, *Turn off the television for a few weeks and spend your evenings in the Word*, don't argue with Him. Just do it. He may tell you to put aside things that aren't sinful, just unnecessary. He may ask you to set aside some hobby or recreational activity and use that time to build up your spirit with the Word of God, because He knows you will need extra strength in the days to come.

Even when you haven't sensed a special prompting of the Lord to spend extra hours in the Word, be faithful to spend some time in it every day. Make abiding in the Word your permanent lifestyle so that His Word can abide in you. Open the way for it to make lasting changes in you and your circumstances by building the truth of it into your spirit day after day. Let it become engrafted in you to such a degree that it becomes a part of you. According to Jesus in John 15:7, you will ask what you will and it will be done. That is a great investment of your time!

That doesn't happen overnight. It takes time.

From the first day Ken and I began to walk by faith, our lives began to improve. But it took awhile for us to lay hold of the Word of God to such an extent that it could significantly change our circumstances. It took time for the Word to work its way down into our hearts, take root there to take over our minds and mouths and then become fruitful.

So don't become impatient. Don't expect to revolutionize your entire life in a day or two. Give the Word time to work. If you do, you will soon begin to see the blessings of God come into your life in a magnificent way.

CHAPTER 10

Abiding Is Obeying

As important as it is to spend time reading, meditating and listening to God's Word, those things alone do not qualify you as one who abides. To be a true "abider" you must take one more step. You must not only hear the Word; you must do it.

Abiding is obeying. "For yourselves, let the teaching which you have heard from the beginning abide within you. If that teaching does abide within you, you also will abide in the Son and in the Father. And this is the promise which He Himself has given us—the life eternal" (1 John 2:24–25, WEYMOUTH).

Jesus said:

> *He that hath my commandments, and keepeth them, he it is that loveth me: and he that loveth me shall be loved of my Father, and I will love him, and will manifest myself to him....If a man love me, he will keep my words: and my Father will love him, and we will come unto him, and make our abode with him....If ye keep my commandments, ye shall abide in my love; even as I have kept my Father's commandments, and abide in his love.... This is my command-*

ment, That ye love one another, as I have loved you. (John
14:21, 23; 15:10, 12)

It is so important to understand that to obey is to abide. There
are many people who claim to know God. They can quote long
passages of Scripture and may have even spent years in seminary
studying the Bible. Yet they are deceived because they are not
doers of the Word. They are hearers only. (See James 1:22.)

The Word that is truly alive in us is not only the Word we know,
but the Word we *do*. First John 2:3–6 says it this way:

> *And hereby we do know that we know him, if we keep his
> commandments. He that saith, I know him, and keepeth not
> his commandments, is a liar, and the truth is not in him. But
> whoso keepeth his word, in him verily is the love of God per-
> fected: hereby know we that we are in him. He that saith
> he abideth in him ought himself also so to walk, even as he
> walked.*

If we're abiding in Jesus, we will live as He lived. How did
He live? In obedience! He was obedient to God in all things.
He wouldn't even say anything except what the Father told Him
to say.

"For I came down from heaven, not to do mine own will, but
the will of him that sent me" (John 6:38). Jesus didn't live for
Himself. He lived to fulfill the Word and plan of His Father. He
lived to be obedient.

Do you know how God responded to that obedience? He gave
Jesus His Spirit without measure. (See John 3:34.) As a result,

Jesus walked the earth in total victory. He defeated Satan and destroyed his works at every turn. Everywhere He went that they received Him, He caused the blind to see, the lame to walk and the deaf to hear. He cast out demons and raised the dead.

The world tries to convince us that it's more exciting to sin than to obey God. But Jesus proved that it is not. He lived the most exciting life in history.

Obeying God will not doom you to a life of boredom. Obeying God will not cheat you out of the good things of life. No! Obedience will lead you into the most thrilling life of victory and blessing you could ever imagine.

God desires to pour His power through you just as He poured it through Jesus. He desires to give you everything you ask for in prayer. He wants to bring to pass in your life the promise Jesus made in John 14:12–15:

> *Verily, verily, I say unto you, He that believeth on me, the works that I do shall he do also; and greater works than these shall he do; because I go unto my Father. And whatsoever ye shall ask in my name, that will I do, that the Father may be glorified in the Son. If ye shall ask any thing in my name, I will do it. If ye love me, keep my commandments.*

All too often, Christians quote those first three verses and leave out the last one. But that won't work. If we want to do the works of Jesus, we must live as He lived. We must abide in Him. And abiding is obeying His commandments.

Go in Love

As we saw in John 15:12, Jesus said, "This is my commandment, That ye love one another, as I have loved you." The Apostle John, while addressing the issue of answered prayer in 1 John 3:21–23, echoes His Words:

> *And, beloved, if our consciences (our hearts) do not accuse us [if they do not make us feel guilty and condemn us], we have confidence (complete assurance and boldness) before God, And we receive from Him whatever we ask, because we [watchfully] obey His orders [observe His suggestions and injunctions, follow His plan for us] and [habitually] practice what is pleasing to Him. And this is His order (His command, His injunction): that we should believe in (put our faith and trust in and adhere to and rely on) the name of His Son Jesus Christ (the Messiah), and that we should love one another, just as He has commanded us.* (AMP)

> *Beloved, if our hearts do not condemn us, we address God with confidence; and whatever we ask for we obtain from Him, because we obey His commands and do what is pleasing in His sight. And this is His command—that we are to believe in the name of His Son Jesus Christ and love one another, as He has commanded us to do.* (WEYMOUTH)

The love of God is our commandment. Obeying that commandment—living a lifestyle of love—is essential if you want to remain in constant fellowship with God. First John 4:16 says, "God is love, and he who dwells and continues in love dwells and continues in God, and God dwells and continues in him" (AMP). Every step out of love is a step out of this vital, daily communion with God.

Years ago Rufus Moseley wrote that if we live by the commandment of love, God's presence will always be with us. He shared his response to a word he received from God:

The answer came... clearly from Him.

"My presence shall go with thee and give thee rest. Go in love and I shall always be with thee."

I knew this was the secret. If we abide in His love and always go in love, feeling and willing and giving out nothing but love and all possible love to all men and all things, we will always be in Him and under His anointing. It was made known to me that I could write editorials and do everything else that can be done in the loving Spirit of Jesus. I could even be in Heavenly places while plowing with a mule, pruning trees, in courtrooms, in death cells, in all places of need, provided all was done in the Spirit of love. It was also clear that one may give all his time to so-called religious work and yet, unless this work is done in the Spirit of Jesus, he will be outside of the Kingdom of God.

It is not what we are doing, but the spirit and motive in which it is done that counts with God. I was made glad and free almost beyond belief. God had simplified everything to me and made sure that Heaven can and will be everywhere as we go in His love, manifesting His love and nothing but

His love. The master key of the Kingdom of Heaven, of abiding union with Jesus, had been given me.[6]

The Master Key

Exactly what is this God kind of love? How does it display itself? First Corinthians 13:4–8 gives us a clear answer to those questions. It says:

> *Love endures long and is patient and kind; love never is envious nor boils over with jealousy, is not boastful or vainglorious, does not display itself haughtily. It is not conceited (arrogant and inflated with pride); it is not rude (unmannerly) and does not act unbecomingly. Love (God's love in us) does not insist on its own rights or its own way, for it is not self-seeking; it is not touchy or fretful or resentful; it takes no account of the evil done to it [it pays no attention to a suffered wrong]. It does not rejoice at injustice and unrighteousness, but rejoices when right and truth prevail.*
>
> *Love bears up under anything and everything that comes, is ever ready to believe the best of every person, its hopes are fadeless under all circumstances, and it endures everything [without weakening]. Love never fails...* (AMP)

As we meditate and act on the revelation of love that comes through these verses, this God-kind of love begins to dominate our thought life and stops every response to meanness, selfishness, every kind of persecution and hurt. God's love shed abroad in our hearts by the Holy Spirit never fails when we respond to it. Thank God for the fruit of our reborn spirit created in His image. If you are born again, you have this wonderful, powerful love on the inside of you. Yield to it and all will be well with you.

You Are Not on Your Own

If you are sitting there thinking you could never consistently live a life of love—that it would simply be too hard for you—don't worry. None of us could do it on our own. But, thank God, we are not on our own! The Greater One is in us. It's His strength within us that makes us victorious.

Because God's own Spirit lives inside us, constantly empowering us to do His will, obedience isn't a burden—it's a joy! First John 5:3–4 confirms that, saying:

> *For the [true] love of God is this: that we do His commands [keep His ordinances and are mindful of His precepts and teaching]. And these orders of His are not irksome (burdensome, oppressive, or grievous). For whatever is born of God is victorious over the world; and this is the victory that conquers the world, even our faith.* (AMP)

If you have chosen Jesus Christ as your Lord, you are an overcomer. You may not be overcoming right now, but you have what it takes on the inside to overcome. So step into that overcoming lifestyle by spending time in the Word developing your faith and spending time in prayer fellowshiping with your Father. As you spend time with Him, you get to know Him better. Talk to Him. Listen to Him. Obey Him. Depend on Him. Become like Him! God is love.

Allow the Word to change how you see yourself. Maybe you've suffered from low self-esteem all your life. Maybe you've been abused or criticized so much that you think of yourself as a failure. If so, stop focusing on yourself and turn your focus on the Word of God instead. Remember what we learned from 1 John 4:4: "Greater is he that is in you, than he that is in the world"! Begin to see yourself as the Father sees you. Whatever He says about you as His child, that's the way it really is. Come into agreement with Him. He's God!

When you abide in the Word of God, you'll be cured of low self-esteem. You won't see yourself in failure any longer. You'll see yourself in God and God in you.

You'll begin to read words like, "Behold, what manner of love the Father hath bestowed upon us, that we should be called the sons of God..." (1 John 3:1). You'll begin to see by revelation of the Spirit that God actually is your Father. He does care for you. You are re-created in Christ Jesus. All those failures of the past have passed away, and all things have become new.

You will realize that you are in God and He is in you. Then, when the devil of low self-esteem comes to you and says, *You'll never be able to obey God. You're not strong enough. You're not able.* You'll answer him and say, "That's right. I'm not able in myself. 'Myself' needs God! And I have Him living here inside me. So get out of the way, devil. I am an overcomer because *the greater one lives in me!* Greater is He that is in me than he that is in the world!" (See 1 John 4:4.)

CHAPTER 11

Developing Confidence in the Holy Spirit

Ye are of God, little children, and have overcome them: because greater is he that is in you, than he that is in the world. (1 John 4:4)

In order to enjoy real day-by-day, moment-by-moment communion and fellowship with God, it is essential that we develop a deeper faith in the Greater One who is living within us. We must cultivate an awesome appreciation for the indwelling Holy Spirit. We must come to see Him like John G. Lake did, as "a reward so great that Jesus Himself considered it worth all His sufferings, all His buffetings, His Earth career, His humiliation, His sacrifice and death. All to obtain it, the GIFT OF THE HOLY SPIRIT."[7]

Jesus obtained the gift of the Holy Spirit for us! The Holy Spirit was the One on whom the disciples were instructed to pin their hope during the dark hours before Jesus' crucifixion. The Holy Spirit was the One Jesus spoke to them about in those last precious moments, saying:

> *Whither I go, thou canst not follow me now; but thou shalt follow me afterwards....And I will pray the Father, and he shall give you another Comforter, that he may abide with you for ever; Even the Spirit of truth; whom the world cannot receive, because it seeth him not, neither knoweth him: but ye know him; for he dwelleth with you, and shall be in you. I will not leave you comfortless: I will come to you....These things have I spoken unto you, being yet present with you. But the Comforter, which is the Holy Ghost, whom the Father will send in my name, he shall teach you all things, and bring all things to your remembrance, whatsoever I have said unto you. (John 13:36; 14:16–18, 25–26)*

To understand the impact of these words, you must realize that for three years, Jesus had been everything to His disciples. He had been their teacher. He had been their provider. When they had moments of fear and weakness, Jesus strengthened them. When they were confused, He counseled them. When they didn't know what to do or where to go, He gave them direction.

Those were the things they had in mind when they heard Him say, "I'm leaving but I'm not leaving you helpless. I'm sending Someone to take My place, Someone to act in My behalf, Someone to do everything for you that I have been doing. It will even be better than having Me here with you in the flesh" (my paraphrase).

No doubt the disciples thought, *How could anyone do for us what You have done, Jesus?* They must have been stunned by sorrow and grief at the prospect of being without Him.

But Jesus didn't share that perspective. He didn't say, "I'm sorry, guys. I know things won't be as good for you after I'm gone, but the Holy Spirit will help you muddle through somehow."

No! Jesus said something far different. He said:

> *Because I have said these things to you, sorrow has filled your hearts [taken complete possession of them]. However, I am telling you nothing but the truth when I say it is profitable (good, expedient, advantageous) for you that I go away. Because if I do not go away, the Comforter (Counselor, Helper, Advocate, Intercessor, Strengthener, Standby) will not come to you [into close fellowship with you]; but if I go away, I will send Him to you [to be in close fellowship with you].* (John 16:6–7, AMP)

Don't ever desire to be like the first disciples. Don't ever think it would be easier to walk in faith if Jesus were physically by your side. He said it's better, more advantageous and more profitable to have the Holy Spirit inside you! You are far better off than the disciples were during Jesus' earthly ministry, for the same Holy Spirit who equipped and empowered Jesus Himself is now resident within you to equip and empower you.

Supernatural Counsel 24 Hours a Day

"Well, Gloria, I just can't see how anything could be better than walking with Jesus on the shores of Galilee like Peter and John did."

Sure you can! Think about it for a moment. When Jesus was on the earth, He had to divide His time between His disciples.

He couldn't be everywhere at once. He couldn't be teaching and counseling each one of them twenty-four hours a day.

But the Holy Spirit can. He can be there when we wake up in the morning, fellowship with us all day long, put us to bed at night and abide in us while we sleep. If we wake up at 2 A.M. with a need or a question, He's there. No matter what time of the day or night we need Him, He's always available to us.

The Holy Spirit dwelling within us is our direct connection to the Father. He enables us to stay in continual fellowship and union with Him. He is the Spirit of the Father. We don't have to go to the high priest to ask for forgiveness. We don't have to go to some clergyman or church building to be in touch with God. We can just go to Him directly, any moment of the day or night. We can stay in contact with heaven all the time.

The Bible says if you are a born-again believer, you are a mobile temple of God! "Your body is the temple (the very sanctuary) of the Holy Spirit who lives within you, whom you have received [as a Gift] from God" (1 Corinthians 6:19, AMP).

What a gift! You never have to wonder, *God, where are You?* You never have to check your feelings to see if God is close to you or a million miles away. You can know He is right there inside you every moment of the day—whether you feel Him or not—because the Word says He is.

He is not just along for the ride, either. He is there to teach you what you need to know and then empower you to walk it out. He's there to be your counselor. And what a wonderful counselor He is! He knows the answer to every problem you'll ever have, and because of that you can have peace, even in the midst of a troubled world.

It doesn't matter how much trouble you're in, you will never ask the Holy Spirit for help and hear Him say, "Oh, I don't know—that's a tough one. You'll have to come back later because you have come up with a problem so complicated that I don't know the answer to it."

No, if you're in trouble, God always has a way out. If you give Him a way into your life, He can provide you with a way out of any problem. You'll never find that He doesn't know what to do.

If you had a human counselor who was that smart—a natural person who knew the answer to every problem you had—you would keep their phone number written on your heart, wouldn't you? If you could just call them every time you ran into trouble and they could tell you what to do to straighten out the situation, you would be on the phone to them a hundred times a day!

Of course, there's no human being with that kind of wisdom and power. But if you are filled with the Holy Spirit, you do have a counselor like that. You have someone who "will guide you into all truth...and he will show you things to come" (John 16:13). You don't even have to call Him on the phone. He's faster than e-mail. He's right there for you all the time. Through Him, any hour of the day or night you always have a living connection with God.

Find Out How God Thinks

Think of the opportunity we have! Through the indwelling Holy Spirit, we have the privilege of fellowshiping with Almighty God—the Most High God with authority over every other power. You can't spend time with the highest authority—the wisest, most loving, the kindest, most generous One in the universe—and not have it affect you greatly. You can't spend time in the presence of the Lord and just stay the same natural person. The more time you give Him, the more you will be like Him. Second Corinthians 3:17–18 says:

Now the Lord is the Spirit, and where the Spirit of the Lord is, there is liberty (emancipation from bondage, freedom). And all of us, as with unveiled face, [because we] continued to behold [in the Word of God] as in a mirror the glory of the Lord, are constantly being transfigured into His very own image in ever increasing splendor and from one degree of glory to another; [for this comes] from the Lord [Who is] the Spirit. (AMP)

Colossians 3:10 says, "Put on the new man, which is renewed in knowledge after the image of him that created him."

Fellowship with God builds you up. It allows you to find out how God thinks. If you'll let Him, the Spirit of God living within your spirit will reveal to you the inside of God—the heart of the Father. He will show you God's plan for your life and then teach you how to walk in that plan step by step. He will give you the wisdom to be a success in every area of your life.

First Corinthians 2:9–10 says:

What eye has not seen and ear has not heard and has not entered into the heart of man, [all that] God has prepared (made and keeps ready) for those who love Him.... Yet to us God has unveiled and revealed them by and through His

Spirit, for the [Holy] Spirit searches diligently, exploring and examining everything, even sounding the profound and bottomless things of God... (AMP)

As amazing as it may seem, those verses clearly tell us that the bottomless things of God are available to every Christian who will spend time with this wonderful Counselor! Yet instead of taking advantage of that privilege, many Christians become busy with natural things. They say, "Oh yes, amen. I know the Holy Spirit lives in me," and then they walk off and act as though He doesn't. They don't give Him any time or attention. They don't spend enough time tuning in to Him through prayer and the Word of God to hear His voice. As a result, they miss His directions.

If you'll learn to be sensitive to the Holy Spirit, He'll help you at the most surprising times. You might just be going about your daily business doing household chores or driving down the street, and suddenly the Spirit of God will move in you and you'll be enlightened. He will tell you something you desperately need to know. What a wonderful blessing!

I remember a crucial time when that happened to me. I was driving home, and as I turned into our neighborhood, the Holy Spirit moved in my heart and a light went on in my spirit. (Proverbs 20:27 says, "The spirit of man is the candle of the Lord...." He gives light to your spirit, so you know which way to go.)

Thou wilt show me the path of life: in thy presence is fulness of joy; at thy right hand there are pleasures for evermore. (Psalm 16:11)

But the path of the [uncompromisingly] just and righteous
is like the light of dawn, that shines more and more (brighter
and clearer) until [it reaches its full strength and glory in]
the perfect day [to be prepared]. (Proverbs 4:18, AMP)

During the previous weeks, Ken and I had been talking with a builder who wanted to develop a subdivision on some of the ministry property. At the time, the ministry needed money; and since we had no immediate plans for that land, selling it seemed a practical thing to do. So we had been praying about it.

Plans had been made. Papers were being drawn up. And, although we hadn't signed anything, the deal was ready to be finalized.

But that day as I was turning into our neighborhood, a light went on in my heart and I received strong direction from the Lord, saying, *Don't you do it! Don't you sell that land!*

It was over in a flash. As far as Ken and I were concerned, that settled the matter. We never again considered that housing development. Even though we desperately needed the money at the time, we just cut off negotiations.

Of course, the money we needed came in through other avenues. God provided for us as He always does, and the ministry still owns the land. What's more, I'm sure the Holy Spirit saved us untold trouble by steering us clear of that situation.

The Only Safe Way to Live

The Holy Spirit is no respecter of persons. He didn't give us that guidance because Ken and I are in the ministry. He gave it to us because we follow Proverbs 3:5–6: "Trust in the Lord with all thine heart; and lean not unto thine own understanding. In all thy ways acknowledge him, and he shall direct thy paths." We asked Him for His will in the matter and expected Him to reveal it to us.

You may say, "I just don't know about that. I don't think I have the kind of connection with God that you do."

Yes, you do, if you're born of God. I'm sure of it because the Apostle John wrote a letter to believers and said, without qualification:

> But as for you, the anointing (the sacred appointment, the unction) which you received from Him abides [permanently] in you; [so] then you have no need that anyone should instruct you. But just as His anointing teaches you concerning everything and is true and is no falsehood, so you must abide in... Him... (1 John 2:27, AMP)

If you are a believer, you have the anointing—or unction—of the Holy Spirit within you. That anointing is there to lead and guide you. If you will maintain a lifestyle of spending time with God and putting His Word in your heart, then the Holy Spirit will talk to you and continually give you the answers and information you need to walk in victory in every area of your life. If you will live in contact with God—listening for His Spirit, being patient to wait on Him until you hear His voice and being pliable and quick to obey when He speaks—He will keep you out of bad situations. He will keep you out of court. He will keep you out of the lawyer's office. He will keep you out of bad business deals and all kinds of other catastrophes.

If you ignore that anointing, however, and just forge ahead making decisions based strictly on your natural intelligence, without praying, seeking and obeying God, too often you'll find yourself in more trouble than you can handle.

It is a wonderful thing to be filled with the Holy Spirit! It's a wonderful thing to be able to hear from heaven about your daily life and to receive supernatural guidance about what to do. But you have to cultivate a hearing heart. You can't just spend your time attending ballgames and watching television and then run to your pastor for prayer and a word of wisdom when you need it. If you've been doing that, stop it. That is nothing more than spiritual laziness, and it will eventually land you in trouble.

Thank God for a good pastor, but you need to start doing your own praying. You shouldn't depend on another person's faith— even if that other person is your pastor. Your pastor is there to help you, and he'll build you up and teach you the Word, but he's not God. As you grow up spiritually, you are able to go to God, pray the prayer of faith and hear from Him yourself.

God didn't give you the Holy Spirit so you could be dependent on someone else. He gave you the Holy Spirit so you could be dependent on Him! So build your life in such a way that you can hear from heaven for yourself. Draw near to God, and He will draw near to you. Learn how to listen to the Counselor and follow Him.

Granted, that will take time and effort, but it is the only safe way to live. After all, the pastor may have more problems than you do. Your needs might not be top priority on his list. He might forget to pray about them, but you won't! Your problems are more important to you than to anyone else on Earth. It's not realistic to expect someone else to have the same interest and fervency that you do.

If you're a new Christian, you may have to depend on others for a while until you have time to develop your own faith. But don't be content to remain a spiritual baby. Get busy. Spend time in the Word and in prayer. Study what the Bible has to say about the Holy Spirit within you. Build your faith in Him. He is God.

Meditate on all the Holy Spirit has been sent to do for you. He has come not only to teach you, but also to show you things to come. As Christians, we should not be in the dark. We ought to know the things that are coming upon the earth. We ought to be like Noah. When all the world around him was in the dark concerning what was about to happen, Noah was hearing from God. The Holy Spirit of God told him what was coming and told him how to plan for it down to the last detail. So when the Flood came, Noah wasn't in the dark—he was in the ark! He and all of his family were saved by hearing and doing what God said.

The Holy Spirit will do the same thing for us if we will just pay attention to Him. He will let us know what's ahead, so we can prepare and continue to do what we are called to do, regardless of what happens to the economy or any other natural situation.

What's more, when we face a hard situation, He will be our Strengthener. When we feel ourselves growing weak and starting to slip into fear or doubt, He will speak to us and give us light from the Word that will make us strong again.

The Amplified Bible says He will also be our Standby. What does that mean? It means He'll be standing by to help when you need it.

Sometimes you will be moving through life just fine, and then you hit a challenge that requires something extra. It's like you're climbing up a mountain and you need a push to help you over the top. The Holy Spirit will give you that extra boost. If you will look to Him in faith, He will help you when the pressure of circumstances becomes too great. His strength and ability are limitless, so He always has whatever you need.

Remember this: Everything Jesus has—and all that He is—is made available to you through the Holy Spirit. You have everything when you are filled with Him. But to enjoy His provision, you must spend time with Him. You must live vitally united to Him, in communion with Him continually.

Learn to commune with the Lord throughout the day. Worship Him. Visit with Him. Sing to Him. Listen to Him. Brother Lawrence, a monk from the 1600s, is still a famous Christian today because He learned to "practice the presence of God," even in everyday tasks and mundane chores. He learned how to walk in the spirit and live in the spirit. We can learn how to do that also if we will give ourselves fully to God by letting the Holy Spirit lead us, teach us, strengthen us and become the most powerful voice in our lives.

CHAPTER 12

Drawing from God's Wise Counsel

The Counselor Himself, the Holy Spirit, lives in your spirit to lead and guide you—but you have to take the time to draw out the deep waters of His counsel.

Nothing should be more precious to us than the counsel of the Lord. That counsel holds the treasures of wisdom, peace, joy and prosperity that we need to walk in the fullness of God's life and blessings. So let's look in Proverbs 20 at some keys to receiving the counsel of the Lord. We'll use those keys to unlock other principles of divine direction!

The Deep Waters of God's Counsel

Let's look at one of those keys: "Counsel in the heart of man is like water in a deep well, but a man of understanding draws it out" (Proverbs 20:5, AMP).

Divine counsel comes to you from your spirit. The Counselor Himself, the Holy Spirit, lives in your spirit, but you have to *draw out* the deep waters of His counsel. *You do that by giving God your attention as you spend time in His Word and in prayer.*

If you are too busy to fellowship with God in the Word and prayer, then all of the hubbub and clamor of daily life can make it extremely difficult to hear the Holy Spirit's counsel in your spirit. You have to take the time to draw that counsel out. You have to listen.

You just can't stay busy with all the distractions of the world and still draw out what God is telling you to do. You have to get quiet in your spirit and listen to Him. When you get quiet and listen, you'll come to a place where you'll just know in your heart that you've received the counsel of the Lord. You will have a "knowing."

The Candle of the Lord

Now let's look at another key verse for further insight into drawing out the Holy Spirit's counsel for our lives: "The spirit of man [that factor in human personality which proceeds immediately from God] is the lamp of the Lord, searching all his innermost parts" (Proverbs 20:27, AMP).

The *King James Version* calls the spirit of man "the *candle* of the Lord."

> *The spirit of man is the candle of the Lord, searching all the inward parts of the belly.*

You see, your spirit is where God's light of revelation comes to you. Out in the natural world that is ruled by darkness, you are surrounded by the lower thoughts of this earthly life. However, God's higher ways and thoughts reside within the deep well of your spirit. He gives you His thoughts, but those thoughts must be drawn out so understanding and wisdom can rise from your spirit and overcome natural knowledge to influence your thoughts.

That's what the psalmist meant when he said, "You cause my lamp to be lighted and shine; the Lord my God illumines my darkness" (Psalm 18:28, AMP). When you face a situation where you have to make a decision but you don't know what to do, God will enlighten your darkness. We even say, "It just dawned on me," because it's as though a light is turned on, the answer is there and suddenly you know what to do. In other words, His counsel guides you in the way of wisdom so you can come through that situation in victory! "The light of the righteous rejoiceth" (Proverbs 13:9).

Jesus said, "Those who follow Me do not walk in darkness" (John 8:12, my paraphrase). As believers we don't ever have to walk in darkness, because the Holy Spirit lights our candle with His revelation and illumines our darkness with the wisdom of God, "once hidden [from the human understanding] and now revealed to us by God" (1 Corinthians 2:7, AMP).

God has put His Spirit on the inside of us to reveal to us all that He has already done for us through Jesus Christ and to give us direction in our personal lives.

It's a sad state of affairs when people get born again, yet never know all that Jesus has wrought for their complete deliverance and salvation. For instance, believers can live their entire lives without learning that Jesus bore their sicknesses and carried their diseases. (See Matthew 8:17.) Many never find out that God's Word promises deliverance from poverty.

In fact, it's not unusual for a person to be born again and still live in poverty, lack and sickness the rest of his life. The only thing that will deliver him from such a fate is God's wisdom and counsel. That's why a wise man of understanding will draw from the deep waters of divine counsel and begin to live a higher way of life than those people just living in the natural realm.

With God's counsel, we can walk with Him in victory when there is turmoil all around us. We can be like the children of Israel.

The Israelites had light shining in their homes when darkness lay on the land of Goshen so thick that no one moved for three days! (See Exodus 10:21–23.) In the same way, the light of God's counsel can shine out of our spirits into a dark and confused world—a world where many people have no idea where they're headed in life.

You see, we aren't limited to what is going on in the natural realm. We can draw out the counsel of God and walk in His higher ways. He knows everything! He knows the past. He knows the future. He knows men's hearts.

We have to let go of the low life to take hold of the high life. We can't hold on to the sin we used to indulge in and still enter into God's realm of light, glory and victory. The Scripture warns us about this: "Whoever curses his father or his mother, his lamp shall be put out in complete darkness" (Proverbs 20:20, AMP). Sin can snuff out the candle of our spirit, making it almost impossible to hear the Holy Spirit when He tries to lead and guide us.

Sin desensitizes us so that we don't hear God speak to us.

Cares of this world, deceitfulness of riches and lusts of other things enter into the heart and choke the Word. *The Amplified Bible* says they "suffocate" the Word. The Word in the heart then becomes "fruitless" or non-productive. (See Mark 4:19.) The less cluttered your heart is, the more sensitive you are to hearing God.

That's why we have to fling those weights and sins aside and take hold of God's counsel. In His higher life are liberty, healing, deliverance and abundance. Drawing from His wise counsel causes us to live continually in the blessings of God. When you live in the blessings, you don't need miracles! Everything is already provided.

God Orders Our Steps

We all need God's counsel to order our steps. That's the only way we're going to make it successfully through life! Proverbs 20:24 (AMP) confirms this: "Man's steps are ordered by the Lord. How then can a man understand his way?"

I learned something interesting about the word "man" in this verse. The first time it's used, the word "man" comes from the Hebrew word *geber,* which means *strong man.* The second time "man" is used, it is translated from the Hebrew word *adam* meaning *ordinary man.*[8] So this scripture actually reads like this: "A *strong man's* steps are ordered by the Lord. How then can an *ordinary man* understand his way?"

We just can't understand life without God. There is nothing to dispel the darkness without His light. We need to draw upon God's strength and counsel from within so He can order our steps! "The steps of a good man are ordered by the Lord: and he delighteth in his way" (Psalm 37:23).

Draw the wise counsel of the Lord from your heart as you would draw water from a well. Wisdom comes from your heart to your head. Spend time in the Word and in prayer, and listen. When you face a situation where you don't know what to do, confess, "God lights my candle and enlightens my darkness!" Make the decision to let go of the low life of the world so you can walk in the light and take hold of the high life of God!

CHAPTER 13

Wellsprings and Rivers—Receiving the Fullness of the Holy Spirit

As you see and understand the vital importance of the Holy Spirit in knowing God, you should realize that the Bible speaks of two distinct experiences with the Holy Spirit that are available to every believer. The first is the entrance of the Holy Spirit into your spirit, which took place the moment you were born again. It was that experience Jesus referred to in John 4:10, 13–14 when He spoke to the woman at the well and said:

> *If thou knewest the gift of God, and who it is that saith to thee, Give me to drink; thou wouldest have asked of him, and he would have given thee living water.... Whosoever drinketh of this [natural] water shall thirst again: But whosoever drinketh of the water that I shall give him shall never thirst; but the water that I shall give him shall be in him a well of water springing up into everlasting life.*

All who have made Jesus Christ the Lord of their lives have a well of life that flows out by the Holy Spirit inside them. They can sense the prompting of that life, and can draw on the wellspring of that living water to meet their own personal needs.

Whenever I think of the supernatural well of water springing up into everlasting life, I think of the water well Ken and I have at our house in Arkansas. It's a good well. In fact, it's a faith well. We had to believe God for it.

When the workmen first began digging it, they stopped about midway down and said, "Mrs. Copeland, there's no point in our digging any farther, because we know there's no water there." I asked them how they knew, and they told me they had run into a certain kind of soil that indicates the well would be dry.

Since I had found a scripture in the Bible that says, "Water for him will be sure" (Isaiah 33:16, AMP), I said, "Keep digging!" They did and sure enough, it turned out to be a very good well. Even in dry weather, it doesn't run dry (unless I forget and leave the hose running).

One thing I have noticed about that well, however, is that it seeks a certain level and stays there. It never overflows. It doesn't rush forth like a river to supply the whole county with water. The well of the spirit born of God has a supply of the Holy Spirit of God or an influence of His Spirit, but there is no overflow—no abundance.

A good picture of this is what happens when you fill a glass with water. That filled glass can take care of your need. But it cannot quench the thirst of the whole town. For that, you will need a supply from God that is more than your well of life. You will need an overflow. That's why He also makes available to you rivers of living water. He does it through the Baptism in the Holy Spirit.

Let the Rivers Flow

Some denominations have taught that the wellspring of the Holy Spirit received at the new birth is all God intends for us to have. But the Bible teaches us that something more is available. John 7:37–39 speaks of that something more, saying:

> *In the last day, that great day of the feast, Jesus stood and cried, saying, If any man thirst, let him come unto me, and drink. He that believeth on me, as the scripture hath said, out of his belly shall flow rivers of living water. (But this spake he of the Spirit, which they that believe on him should receive: for the Holy Ghost was not yet given; because that Jesus was not yet glorified.)*

Notice, Jesus didn't mention a well. He didn't talk about a spring. He talked about rivers! He was talking about ministering to others.

Think about it this way: A well just sits there, but a river takes its course wherever it wants to go. A river is powerful. A river has much more water than a well. And it doesn't just belong to one person—it's there for everyone. It supplies water to multitudes.

God never intended for us as believers to have just enough of the Holy Spirit to take care of ourselves personally. It is His will for us to be overflowing with His power. It is His will for us to live in such outstanding victory that we are living demonstrations to the multitudes that Jesus is alive! He wants rivers of the Spirit flowing through us, so we can cast out devils, speak with new tongues, and lay hands on the sick and see them recover. (See Mark 16:17–18.)

In other words, God wants us to receive the Baptism in the Holy Spirit just as the first disciples did, so we can act just like they acted! So we can obey the words of Jesus. "I assure you, most solemnly I tell you, if anyone steadfastly believes in Me, he will himself be able to do the things that I do; and he will do even greater things than these, because I go to the Father" (John 14:12, AMP).

Jesus ascended to the Father and made it possible for us to receive the Baptism in the Holy Spirit! After His death and resurrection, it is that baptism of which He spoke in the book of Acts:

> *And, being assembled together with them, [Jesus] commanded them that they should not depart from Jerusalem, but wait for the promise of the Father, which, saith he, ye have heard of me. For John truly baptized with water; but ye shall be baptized with the Holy Ghost not many days hence. . . . But ye shall receive power, after that the Holy Ghost is come upon you: and ye shall be witnesses unto me both in Jerusalem, and in all Judaea, and in Samaria, and unto the uttermost part of the earth. And when he had spoken these things, while they beheld, he was taken up; and a cloud received him out of their sight. (Acts 1:4–5, 8–9)*

Look again at verse 8: "But ye shall receive power. . . ." The word translated "power" here is the same word translated "virtue" in Luke 8:46. When the woman with an issue of blood touched the hem of Jesus' garment, He said, "Somebody hath touched me: for I perceive that virtue [power] is gone out of me" (Luke 8:46).

That same power—that same equipping and anointing for ministry in which He ministered—is what Jesus promised His disciples (including you and me) would receive when baptized in the Holy Spirit. You no longer have a glass that is full. You have a pitcher that is constantly overflowing—one you can pour without being concerned it will run dry. Now you have an unending supply of life flowing from inside you out into your world.

That's the way God baptizes in the Holy Spirit. He comes from inside of you and overflows with whatever you need to carry out His directions.

The Baptism in the Holy Spirit is your equipping—your anointing—for ministry. And it's not a well. It is rivers that will begin to flow out of you to destroy yokes and remove burdens. That's what happened in the lives of the disciples of Jesus.

These disciples were already born again. Jesus had already breathed on them after His resurrection and said, "Receive ye the Holy Ghost" (John 20:22). That's when they were born again, but that was not enough. Jesus said they needed something more. They needed to be baptized with the Holy Spirit. They needed power—not just the Spirit *within,* but the Spirit *upon.* They needed to be anointed with the Holy Spirit and power.

My, what a change occurred when they received the power of the Holy Spirit! This group that had been so weak and confused during the crucifixion and that had been so afraid that the Jews would come after them, came bursting out of the upper room with boldness and power, speaking with tongues as the Spirit gave them utterance.

Among them was Peter, who just a few weeks earlier had been so afraid of persecution that he'd denied even knowing Jesus. Yet, once baptized in the Holy Spirit, he had the spiritual boldness to point at the same people he had once feared and say:

> *Ye men of Israel, hear these words; Jesus of Nazareth, a man approved of God among you by miracles and wonders and signs, which God did by him in the midst of you, as ye yourselves also know: Him, being delivered by the determinate counsel and foreknowledge of God, ye have taken, and by wicked hands have crucified and slain: Whom God hath raised up.... Repent, and be baptized every one of you in the name of Jesus Christ for the remission of sins, and ye shall receive the gift of the Holy Ghost. For the promise is unto you, and to your children, and to all that are afar off, even as many as the Lord our God shall call.* (Acts 2:22–24, 38–39)

The Baptism in the Holy Spirit Is for All

Some people have said the Baptism in the Holy Spirit was just for those first disciples. But that's not what Peter said. He said it's for all—for you and your children. "For the promise [of the Holy Ghost] is unto you, and to your children, and to all that are afar off, even as many as the Lord our God shall call" (Acts 2:39). That means it is for you and me. If you will read through the book of Acts, you will see this confirmed repeatedly. Again and again, you will see the new believers in the early Church receiving the Baptism in the Holy Spirit after they were born again. In the Scripture it is obviously a separate and distinct experience available to those who have been born again.

In Acts 8:14–17, for example, Philip went to Samaria and preached the gospel to the people there. Many were born again and baptized in water. The Samaritans, however, did not automatically receive the Baptism in the Holy Spirit when they were born again. They received it at a later time.

> Now when the apostles which were at Jerusalem heard that Samaria had received the word of God, they sent unto them Peter and John: Who, when they were come down, prayed for them, that they might receive the Holy Ghost: (For as yet he was fallen upon none of them: only they were baptized in the name of the Lord Jesus.)
> Then laid they their hands on them, and they received the Holy Ghost.

We find a similar occurrence recorded in Acts 19:2–6 where Paul, during his missionary travels, came upon some disciples of John the Baptist in Ephesus:

> [Paul] said unto them, Have ye received the Holy Ghost since ye believed? And they said unto him, We have not so much as heard whether there be any Holy Ghost. And he said unto them, Unto what then were ye baptized? And they said, Unto John's baptism. Then said Paul, John verily baptized with the baptism of repentance, saying unto the people, that they should believe on him which should come after him, that

is, on Christ Jesus. When they heard this, they were baptized in the name of the Lord Jesus. And when Paul had laid his hands upon them, the Holy Ghost came on them; and they spake with tongues, and prophesied.

Notice once again the two separate experiences. These people first believed on Jesus and were baptized in water in His Name (the new birth). Then Paul laid hands on them and they received the Baptism in the Holy Spirit.

The Value of Praying in Tongues

Although these two experiences do not *always* occur at the same time, they can. And it is most wonderful when they do. In Acts 10 when the Gospel was first preached by Peter to the Gentiles, that is what happened. Although Peter did not lay hands on these people, they clearly received both the new birth and the Baptism in the Holy Spirit as Peter was preaching to them about Jesus:

While Peter yet spake these words, the Holy Ghost fell on all them which heard the word. And they of the circumcision which believed were astonished, as many as came with Peter, because that on the Gentiles also was poured out the gift of the Holy Ghost. For they heard them speak with tongues, and magnify God. Then answered Peter, Can any man forbid water, that these should not be baptized, which have received the Holy Ghost as well as we? (Acts 10:44–47)

It is important to note that in this instance, as in those recorded in Acts 2, 8 and 19, which we have already discussed, it is either stated outright or clearly implied that all those who received the Baptism in the Holy Spirit gave evidence of their experience by speaking in tongues.[9] The same is true today. Speaking in tongues is the outward evidence of the Baptism in the Holy Spirit.

Some Christians are uncomfortable with that. "Do I have to speak in tongues?" they ask.

No, you don't *have* to—you get to! Speaking in tongues is not some spiritual badge of honor. It is an indispensable tool that God has given you to help you live a victorious and powerful life. It is a tool you desperately need.

As believers still living in natural bodies, you and I need to be able to pray in tongues because we have weaknesses. Our understanding of spiritual things is limited. We don't yet know all we need to know, and that lack of knowledge can constantly hinder our ability to pray according to the will of God. God has made provision that enables us to overcome that weakness. Romans 8:26–27 describes that provision:

> So too the [Holy] Spirit comes to our aid and bears us up in our weakness; for we do not know what prayer to offer nor how to offer it worthily as we ought, but the Spirit Himself goes to meet our supplication and pleads in our behalf with unspeakable yearnings and groanings too deep for utterance. And He who searches the hearts of men knows what is in the mind of the [Holy] Spirit [what His intent is], because the Spirit intercedes and pleads [before God] in behalf of the saints according to and in harmony with God's will. (AMP)

First Corinthians 14:2 further describes this process, saying, "For he that speaketh in an unknown tongue speaketh not unto men, but unto God: for no man understandeth him; howbeit in the spirit he speaketh mysteries."

You and I need to be praying about what will happen to us tomorrow. We need to be praying about God's plan for us and our families five years from now. We need to be praying out the plan of God for the earth. But many times we don't know those things. They are mysteries to us. What can we do? Pray in other tongues!

Praying in other tongues, or in the spirit, enables you to pray the perfect will of God for your life. It allows you to step out of the realm of the flesh and into the realm of the spirit so that no matter how weak or ignorant you may be in the natural, you can pray exactly as you need to pray, as the Spirit gives you utterance.

Sometimes you will have an insight, a word, an interpretation of what you are praying in the spirit. Say to the Lord, "The things I know not, teach me, and the things I see not, show me." You will begin to receive revelation on things you have never before understood. That's what you need—revelation from God! That's what we all need. The result of praying in tongues might come to you later as "a knowing"—you'll just know something. You will have a word of knowledge from the Spirit of God. (See 1 Corinthians 12:8.) God has things that are so much better for us than what we have seen, that we can't even figure them out. But if we'll pray in the spirit, in other tongues, we will reach beyond our knowledge and expectation, into the area that is "above all that we ask or think" (Ephesians 3:20).

Is it any wonder that speaking in tongues has undergone such persecution? The devil hates it! He knows it is the only way believers can pray beyond what they know and into the limitless possibilities of the Spirit of God.

He understands, even if we don't, that even baby Christians— newly reborn ones—can pray in tongues, receive the mind of the Spirit and start growing fast. That's the way the church at Jerusalem grew in the early days. That's all they had. They couldn't take their New Testaments and read the epistles of John or Paul's letter to the Ephesians. They had to use the ability and understanding the Holy Spirit gave them. And when they did, they turned the whole world upside down. Study the entire chapter of 1 Corinthians 14 concerning this.

Build Yourself Up By Praying

You and I can have the spiritual strength it takes to turn our world upside down for Jesus, if we'll just commit ourselves to spend time each day praying in the spirit. It will not only enlighten us, but it will enable us to overcome the weakness of our flesh.

Our flesh-and-blood bodies haven't been reborn as our spirit has. If you don't take control of your body, it will take you from one failure to another. So you must build up your spirit, strengthen it to the point that it can dominate, or rule over, your flesh.

Praying in the spirit helps us do that. As Jude 20 says, "But you, beloved, build yourselves up [founded] on your most holy faith [make progress, rise like an edifice higher and higher], praying in the Holy Spirit" (AMP).

Praying in the spirit will pump you up like a spiritual body builder. It will enable you to walk in the power of the Spirit instead of the weakness of the flesh.

Prayer of any kind—whether it's in the spirit or with the understanding—is an absolute necessity if you want to be spiritually strong and ready in times of crisis.

In Luke 21:36, Jesus said, "Watch ye therefore, and pray always, that ye may be accounted worthy..." or as *The Amplified Bible* says, "that you may have the full strength and ability...to escape all these things...that will take place...."

If you want to have the strength and ability to come through troubled times in triumph, you'd better spend time in prayer. That's what Jesus urged Peter and the other disciples to do in the Garden of Gethsemane. He knew they were about to face one of the toughest times of their lives. He said, "Watch ye and pray, lest ye enter into temptation. The spirit truly is ready, but the flesh is weak" (Mark 14:38).

Instead of obeying Jesus' admonition to pray, the Scripture tells us the disciples went to sleep. In Peter's life, in particular, we can see the result. When temptation came, he entered into it and denied the Lord.

You might as well face it. Temptation will come to you as long as you live in a flesh body. So you'd better stay prayed up! Tests will come as long as we live in the flesh, but we can pass them if we will obey our born-again spirit and not our flesh. After all, it is an open-book test!

I remember when God first began revealing to me about the importance of praying in the spirit. I had been asking Him to show me how to quit living so much on the natural, circumstantial level and start walking more in the spirit.

I had been committed to the Word for years at that time. I regularly spent much time reading and meditating on it, and that alone had already revolutionized my life. But I knew there was still something lacking.

God showed me that I needed to increase my prayer time. And He spoke to me specifically about praying in other tongues. Today I can understand why. When I began to pray more in tongues, I began to give my spirit more outflow. I gave vent to it. I became spiritually stronger. It completely changed me. I am so different now than I was before, and I'm still changing!

Giving place to your spirit is the way you walk in the spirit, just like giving place to your flesh is the way you walk in the flesh. The more I released my spirit by praying in other tongues, the more my spirit began to take charge. I found it worked just as the Bible says—if you "walk in the spirit . . . ye shall not fulfil the lust of the flesh" (Galatians 5:16). I found it easier to hear and obey my spirit indwelt by the Holy Spirit.

Isn't that simple? The devil has tried to hide the simplicity of it from us because he knows if we ever start doing it, he'll have no place left. He's limited. He can't touch your reborn spirit. The only thing he has to work on is your flesh. Learn what brings the flesh under dominion. Once you learn that praying in the spirit applies spirit to flesh and causes the flesh to obey God the way it should, the devil won't be able to obtain a foothold in your life at all! Rivers of the Spirit will start flowing out of you to change things supernaturally! Your spirit will begin to dominate your flesh.

How to Receive the Baptism in the Holy Spirit

If you haven't yet received the Baptism in the Holy Spirit—if you have never prayed in other tongues—I urge you not to let one more day go by without doing so. It isn't difficult. To qualify for it, the only condition you must meet is that you make Jesus Christ the Lord of your life. You must be born again.

Once you have met that condition, the Baptism in the Holy Spirit is yours for the asking. You don't have to be afraid that you won't receive it or that you will receive some evil counterfeit, for Jesus said:

> *For every one that asketh receiveth; and he that seeketh findeth; and to him that knocketh it shall be opened. If a son shall ask bread of any of you that is a father, will he give him a stone? or if he ask a fish, will he for a fish give him a serpent? Or if he shall ask an egg, will he offer him a scorpion? If ye then, being evil, know how to give good gifts unto your children: how much more shall your heavenly Father give the Holy Spirit to them that ask him?* (Luke 11:10–13)

To receive the Baptism in the Holy Spirit, all you have to do is ask and, in simple faith, receive. Simply lift your heart to God and say:

> *Father, I come to You now in the Name of Jesus. I have received Jesus as my Savior and the Lord of my life, and I stand before You now, cleansed by the precious blood He shed for me. Lord, You said in Your Word that the promise of the Holy Spirit is for me. So in faith I take You at Your Word. I ask You to baptize me and fill me to overflowing with Your own precious Holy Spirit. Thank You, Lord, for fulfilling Your promise to me. I fully expect now for the Holy Spirit to rise up within me as I pray and give me utterance in other tongues.*

After you have prayed, give expression to your faith by lifting your heartfelt thanks and praises to God. But instead of speaking in your own language, allow the language of the Spirit to flow from within you.

Do not wait for the Holy Spirit to make you speak, because He will not do so. Nowhere does the Bible teach that the Holy Spirit does the speaking. It is the believers themselves who speak. The Holy Spirit supplies the language as we begin to speak out by faith. He gives us utterance.

Don't be concerned with what the words sound like to you. In fact, don't concentrate on the words at all. Just focus your attention on the Lord. Think about how much you love Him. Think about how wonderful and loving and kind He is. Think about the matchless privilege of having a living connection with Him. As you do, just rejoice and trust Him, and although you may feel you are stuttering or stumbling at first, relax in the confidence that God will perfect your praise. (See Matthew 21:16.)

I'll warn you in advance, the devil will probably try to harass you. He may tell you you're silly to speak words you don't understand. If that doesn't work, he may tell you you're not smart enough to speak words you don't understand. When he does, just remember this: Every born-again believer—from the least to the greatest—can pray in other tongues. You don't have to be smart to do it. But, without a doubt, if you'll shove aside those devilish doubts and persist in communing and fellowshiping with God by praying in tongues every day, eventually it will prove to be one of the smartest things you have ever done.

Now you can say, according to 1 John 4:

I do not believe every spirit, but try (test) the spirits, whether they are of God; because many false prophets have gone out into the world.

By this I know the Spirit of God: Every spirit that confesses that Jesus Christ has come in the flesh is of God, and every spirit that does not confess that Jesus Christ has come in the flesh is not of God. And this is the spirit of the antichrist, which I have heard was coming, and is now already in the world.

I am of God and have overcome them, because He who is in me is greater than he who is in the world. They are of the world; therefore, they speak as of the world, and the world hears them. I am of God. He who knows God hears me; he who is not of God does not hear me. By this I know the spirit of truth and the spirit of error.

I love others, for love is of God, and everyone who loves is born of God and knows God. He who does not love does not know God, for God is love. In this the love of God was manifested toward me, that God sent His only begotten Son into the world, that I might live through Him. In this is love, not that I loved God, but that He loved me and sent His Son to be the propitiation for my sins. If God so loved me, I also ought to love others.

No one has seen God at any time. If I love others, God dwells in me, and His love has been perfected in me. By this I know that I dwell in Him, and He in me, because He has given me of His Spirit.

And I have seen and testify that the Father sent the Son

to be the Savior of the world. Whoever confesses that Jesus is the Son of God, God dwells in him, and he in God. And I have known and believed the love that God has for me. God is love, and he who dwells in love dwells in God, and God in him.

Love has been perfected in me in this: that I may have boldness in the Day of Judgment; because as He is, so am I in this world. There is no fear in love; but perfect love casts out fear, because fear involves torment. But he who fears has not been made perfect in love. I love Him because He first loved me.

If someone says, "I love God," and hates his brother, he is a liar; for he who does not love his brother whom he has seen, how can he love God whom he has not seen? And this commandment I have from Him: that he who loves God must love his brother also.

Hallelujah!

CHAPTER 14

Staying Connected to Heaven

Perhaps the greatest challenge we face as Spirit-filled believers is learning to accurately distinguish the leading of the Holy Spirit. It is not an easy task, because when we begin, we are such carnal thinkers. But it is definitely worthwhile, because if we are to abide in the Lord and to maintain a living connection with Him, we must be able to hear and obey the leading of His Spirit. God has always expected His people to do that. When you read the Hebrew covenant, you will see that God told Israel not only to obey His written Word, but also to obey His voice. (See Jeremiah 7:23.) He wanted them to know His will in specific situations.

When the army of Israel invaded Jericho, they must have heard God's voice. Where else would they have acquired the strange battle plan they used? It wasn't written in the Law of Moses. And certainly, no human being would suggest a seven-day march around a city as the most effective form of invasion!

No, that was God's plan. He revealed it to Joshua, and when Joshua followed it, there was victory. For us to walk in victory today, we must do the same thing Joshua did. Not only must we obey the written Word, we must also be able to hear and obey

God's instructions to us about the choices and decisions we face each day.

Say, for example, you are offered a job in another city. Naturally speaking, it may seem to be a great opportunity. It might involve an increase in pay or a promotion. But to be sure what to do, you need guidance from the Lord.

You can open the Bible and receive some general instructions that may help you. But the written Word of God will not tell you whether to take that job or not. You won't find a chapter and verse that says, "Yes, that's a good move. Go to Chicago next May and take the job there. That's God's will for you."

To find out what choice is right in such situations, you must be able to discern the voice or the promptings of the Holy Spirit. You must be sensitive to His leadings in your heart.

How do you cultivate that kind of discernment and sensitivity? In several ways.

The first two, which we've already addressed at length, are to pray daily—both in your own language and in other tongues—and to meditate on the written Word of God. The more familiar you are with God's voice as it comes through the written Word, the more easily you will be able to recognize His voice in your own heart. Through the written Word, your mind becomes renewed to accept God's way as the right thing to do.

Another major key to developing and maintaining spiritual sensitivity is to stay connected to the realm of the spirit throughout the day. Don't just have your daily time in prayer and the Word and then barrel through the rest of your day and forget all about God. Stay tuned in to Him. Think of God often and give Him praise. Consult with Him about things that come up during your day. Pray in tongues on and off throughout the day. Carry around a pocket New Testament with you and take a "Word break" instead of a coffee break.

Throughout the day, keep yourself available to God. Whether you're a business person sitting at a desk or a homemaker buying groceries and cleaning the house—whatever your job is—maintain an awareness and living connection with God so that at any moment, He can reach you if He needs to let you know something.

It is possible to keep your mind so stayed on God that no matter what you come up against, you're just one moment away from hearing from the Holy Spirit. If you will maintain your union with God throughout the day by making Him the number one priority and continually walking in love, you can stay connected to heaven twenty-four hours a day. You can rest in the assurance that you have all of heaven's resources backing you and that the Holy Spirit is constantly with you, ready to talk to you about anything you need to know.

Remember, however, that the Holy Spirit is a gentleman. He won't force Himself on you. If you want Him to be active in your life, you must give Him place. You must be constantly looking to Him for guidance, instead of managing your life according to your own natural plans and ideas.

I have a friend who operates in a great supernatural ministry. He prayed for years that the Spirit of God would manifest Himself in his meetings. Finally, one day the Lord answered him and said, "You don't give Me any opportunity!" In other words, my friend had his agenda and he was not leaving any time or space for the Spirit of God to move.

We've all done that at times. In our meetings and our churches, we have such a habit of doing certain things—of singing a set number of songs, receiving the offering at a particular time and preaching a certain way—that we shut out the Holy Spirit. When my friend realized that was what he was doing, he changed some things.

We need to do the same, not just in our corporate services, but in our individual lives as well. We need to slow down a little and invite the Holy Spirit to interrupt our neat, little plans if He wants to. If we don't make a place for Him, He will not push His way in.

He won't come in while you're sitting on the couch watching television, slap the remote out of your hand and say, "Shut that thing off! I have something to tell you and I can't get a word in edgewise!"

No, He normally just doesn't do that. You have to make place for Him. He will not take over your life. He will wait for you to draw near to Him, and when you do, He'll draw near to you.

So, purpose to draw near to Him throughout the day. When you're in your car, for instance, instead of listening to talk radio, put in a teaching tape or CD and listen to the Word of God. When you're dressing for work, instead of listening to secular music, spend that time singing songs to the Lord and praising Him.

Little things like that can make a great difference in your day. I know that from experience. Some mornings when I wake up, I would rather do almost anything than go into the television studio and tape the daily broadcast. But as I prepare to go to the studio, I'll play a praise tape or just begin to worship God. By the time I arrive at the studio, I'll be singing and praising God. My heart will be lifted and strong and I'll be ready to preach!

Learn to take advantage of such times throughout your day. Take a few minutes here and there to keep yourself strong and built up in the Lord.

Be Available

If you will continue to be faithful to maintain that kind of sensitivity to the Holy Spirit, you will be amazed at what God can do for you and through you. He will enable you to do greater things than you have ever imagined. He will enable you to live like an overcomer and be a blessing to many, many people.

You may not think you have the ability to do anything of consequence. But that doesn't bother God. He isn't looking for ability. He is looking for availability! All He needs is faithfulness.

I suppose it would be wonderful to have great natural talent. But when you connect with God, it doesn't really matter whether you're talented or not. God has all the talent and ability He needs. He doesn't necessarily search out a shining star at some major university and say, "Look at that guy! He is such a wonderful speaker. I think he would make Me a good preacher."

That rarely ever happens. God is much more likely to seek out someone like Oral Roberts. When God called him, he was a seventeen-year-old boy who stuttered so badly that he could hardly say his own name. He was weak and sick, dying of tuberculosis. But he was available. So God cured him of stuttering, healed his body and made him one of the most outstanding healing evangelists of all time.

If you will remain constant in your fellowship with the Lord, it won't matter what you are in the natural. You may be poor or uneducated. You may be the biggest failure on your block. But those things just make you a prime candidate for the calling of God. As the Apostle Paul wrote:

Because the foolishness of God is wiser than men; and the weakness of God is stronger than men. For ye see your calling, brethren, how that not many wise men after the flesh, not many mighty, not many noble, are called: But God hath chosen the foolish things of the world to confound the wise; and God hath chosen the weak things of the world to confound the things which are mighty; And base things of the world, and things which are despised, hath God chosen, yea, and things which are not, to bring to nought things that are: That no flesh should glory in his presence.

But of him are ye in Christ Jesus, who of God is made unto us wisdom, and righteousness, and sanctification, and redemption: That, according as it is written, He that glorieth, let him glory in the Lord. (1 Corinthians 1:25–31)

The new birth is the great equalizer. It takes you out of your natural station in life—whether it is low or high—and puts you in the Anointed Jesus and His Anointing. It makes available to you the wisdom and ability of God Himself. As you give yourself to Him, He will cause that ability to flow through you by anointing you with His Spirit to do whatever He wants you to do.

It thrills me to know that I don't have to be special to be used by God. I just have to be faithful. I just have to yield myself to Him and stay in constant fellowship with Him. To me, that's a tremendous encouragement.

Cultivate an Attitude of Dependency

Actually, I think one of the things that has helped me most has been my awareness of my own natural inadequacy. From the moment God called Ken and me into ministry, I have been aware that I was in over my head. I knew I did not have the ability in the natural to do what God was telling us to do.

Some people feel self-sufficient. They think they are smart enough or talented enough to do things on their own. And though they may have some good results, they'll never see the kinds of supernatural results they would if they were dependent on God.

For me, however, self-sufficiency isn't much of a temptation. In the ministry, everything you have to do is impossible with men, so I have to begin every day dependent on the Holy Spirit. I rarely do anything in the morning before I pray. I like to connect with God first thing in the morning. I like to talk to Him about the things I will face that day. If I have a business meeting, I want to know what He has to say about the issues we'll be discussing at that meeting. I don't want to go in there and be dependent on natural knowledge. If I am ministering, I have to be anointed by His Spirit, or I might as well stay home.

As far as I'm concerned, I can't afford to step out of my house before I've spent time with God.

Actually, the same is true for you. Even if you aren't in the five-fold ministry, as a believer you're called to do impossible things. You are called to lay hands on the sick, for example, and deliver the healing power of God. I don't care how smart and talented you are; you can't do that without depending on the Holy Spirit.

If you are ever tempted to think you can, remember this: Even

Jesus had to depend on the Holy Spirit to carry out His ministry. Although He was the sinless Son of God, He never did a single miracle until the Holy Spirit came upon Him.

What's more, even after His baptism in the Holy Spirit, Jesus said, "I am able to do nothing from Myself [independently, of My own accord—but only as I am taught by God and as I get His orders]. Even as I hear, I judge [I decide as I am bidden to decide. As the voice comes to Me, so I give a decision], and My judgment is right (just, righteous), because I do not seek or consult My own will [I have no desire to do what is pleasing to Myself, My own aim, My own purpose] but only the will and pleasure of the Father Who sent Me" (John 5:30 AMP). Jesus Himself could only live and minister in victory by living in total dependence on God.

Jesus walked out His earthly life just the way you and I are called to walk out our earthly lives. He would continually abide in the Father and His Words, be obedient and hear from heaven about what to do. Jesus didn't live unto Himself. He lived every moment hearing from the Father and obeying Him.

If you will look at Jesus' ministry, you will find that His prayer life was amazing. He would minister to people all day long, and then He would spend all night long alone with God. Why did He do that? Because He was completely dependent on God. Jesus knew He had to receive direction and instructions from the Holy Spirit if He was to do what God had called Him to do.

If that was true for Jesus, it is true for you too! So follow His example and cultivate an attitude of dependency on the Holy Spirit. Ask the Holy Spirit to help you develop such a habit of dependence on Him that it would be unusual for you to go more than fifteen or twenty minutes without talking to Him and looking to Him for assistance.

Heed the instructions in Colossians 2:6 and "just as you trusted Christ [the Anointed One and His Anointing] to save you, trust him, too, for each day's problems; live in vital union with him" (TLB). In other words, depend on Him to help you through the things that you face in your life. Become so Holy Ghost-minded that when a pain or symptom of sickness tries to attach itself to your body, the first thing you think about is not your doctor—but the Word of God and the power of His Spirit. Become so dependent on Him that when you encounter financial trouble, you won't run to your banker first—you'll run to Him.

The more you depend on the Holy Spirit, the more you will open the door for Him to be active in your life. It's your dependency upon Him that clears the way for Him to move. So don't try to make decisions by yourself—because you don't know the future. Lean on the Holy Spirit. He knows what's ahead.

Every day, acknowledge your dependency on Him. Say something like this:

Lord, I am so grateful for the Holy Spirit, who lives in me and teaches me the things I need to know. I'm so grateful He is dwelling in me to be my Guide in every situation and to lead me into all truth. I'm totally dependent upon You, Lord. I am just like a little child. I don't know whether to come in or go out unless You show me what to do. And I am glad to be that way because I love You and trust You with my whole heart.

Help me to walk closely with You all day long. Teach me to live and walk in the spirit—not just when I'm in trouble, but every moment, in union and communion with You.

I trust in the Lord with all my heart and lean not to my own understanding. I acknowledge You in all my ways, and You shall direct my path according to Your Word. In Jesus' Name, I expect to receive guidance today. Thank You, Father, for helping me and directing me. (See Proverbs 3:5–6)

CHAPTER 15

Expect to Be Led by the Spirit

When I refer to hearing from the Spirit of God, you might say, "I can't hear God! He just doesn't speak to me like He speaks to you."

If that is the case with you, there are several possible reasons for it. You may be hindered because you haven't been spending enough time with Him to be sensitive to His promptings or His voice.

You may also be blocking your ability to hear with unbelief. Jesus said plainly, "My sheep hear my voice..." (John 10:27). Therefore, if you are a born-again child of God, you not only *can* but also you *should expect* to hear God speaking to you. To say you cannot hear Him is to doubt the words of Jesus Himself, so don't do it. Instead, use your words to express your faith. Say, "I can hear from God! I know I can because Jesus said so! His sheep know His voice." If you will begin to believe and confess the scriptures about being led by the Lord, you will begin to discern His leadership and distinguish His guidance.

It's likely that you are already hearing from God, but you aren't recognizing it because you are listening for the wrong thing. Often people expect God to speak to them forcefully. They are looking for a burning bush or listening for an audible voice, but normally God speaks to us in less dramatic ways.

His leadings are usually very subtle. They rise up in your heart like holy suggestions. When you sense those "suggestions," you may even wonder, *Was that me, Lord, or was that You?* That's because God doesn't normally inject thoughts directly into your mind from the outside. Instead, He impresses or enlightens your spirit, and your spirit translates that impression into a thought. So when you receive it, it sounds like you. It *was* you! It was your spirit being influenced by the Spirit of God within you.

Such Holy Spirit impressions hardly ever come in and over-whelm you. Most often they come in the form of an inward wit-ness or a quiet inner prompting or a knowing—you just suddenly know something you didn't know before. Romans 8:16 gives us an example of how that inner witness works. There the Apostle Paul says, "The Spirit itself [or Himself] beareth witness with our spirit, that we are the children of God."

If I were to ask if you know you are one of God's children, no doubt you would answer with a quick sure yes! But what would you say if I were to ask you how you know that you are?

You might answer, "I don't know how I know. I just know!"

What you would actually be saying to me is that the Holy Spirit within you bears witness, or gives assurance to your own spirit, and lets you know that you indeed belong to God.

The inward witness, or promptings of the Spirit, work much that same way in the other affairs of life. You might be going about your day just doing your normal activities and suddenly you'll think, *I need to call Aunt Sally.* You may dismiss the thought at first because you're busy doing other things, but then it recurs. *I need to call Aunt Sally,* you'll think again.

Then you may notice that even though calling Aunt Sally wasn't on your agenda for today, it just seems like a good thing to do right now. So you pick up the phone and dial her number. Very likely, you will find out that Aunt Sally was discouraged or in need, and your call came just at the right time. Why? Because you yielded to the prompting of the Holy Spirit.

If you will learn to live each day always listening to your heart for that inner witness, constantly expecting to be prompted by the Spirit of God, you'll find yourself doing things like that quite often. Sometimes you won't even realize you are hearing from heaven. You'll just think you had a good idea, but later you will see that you were responding to the Holy Spirit.

I know of one man, for example, who was living in Oakland, California, and working in San Francisco many years ago when there was a major earthquake. He was sitting in his office just a few hours before that quake when suddenly he had the thought that he should leave work early, so he could avoid the evening traffic that would be heavy due to the World Series ballgame being held nearby.

It seemed like a purely natural thought at the time, but it seemed good to him. In other words, his heart bore witness with it. So he left early to drive home. Just a few hours later, at the time he normally would have been driving home, the very freeway he would have been on collapsed in the earthquake.

Staying in vital communion with God can save your life!

A Sensitivity You Maintain

If you want to have those kinds of experiences, you will have to learn how to listen to your heart as you go about your day. You will have to learn how to hear the still, small voice on the inside of you—in spite of the bustle and noise on the outside of you!

To do that requires diligence and commitment. It takes commitment to put God first place in your life every single day. It takes a determination to daily spend time in the Word and in prayer no matter what!

Why is that time so important? Because hearing from God is not as much a skill you learn as it is a sensitivity you maintain. You can be full of knowledge about how to hear God's leadings. You may have heard them thousands of times before. But if you want to hear today, you must be in communion and fellowship with Him today. You must maintain fellowship with Him on a continual basis.

It is not enough just to go to church on Sundays. You have to stay in touch with God all the time. With the help of the Holy Spirit, you have to rid your life of things you know are displeasing to God, so your communion with Him will not be hindered. Stay full of the Word of God so that your faith will be strong and your spirit will be receptive to His directions. Be constantly looking to and listening for Him so that when He speaks, you hear Him. Otherwise, you may miss out on those gentle promptings He gives you. You will be so occupied with your own plans and activities that you won't pay attention to the witness of the Holy Spirit inside.

When you do sense a leading of the Spirit, when you do begin to discern His voice, it is important to obey the instructions in Hebrews 3:15. "To day if ye will hear his voice, harden not your [heart]...." That means don't resist the promptings of the Spirit.

If you sense He is directing you to do something and you decide—consciously or unconsciously—*No, I don't want to do that. I think I'll go another way,* then you have just hardened your heart. Most of the time, that's how we miss the will of God. We are not trying to be rebellious; it's just that in one situation or another, we don't follow His leading in our spirit. Our natural mind tells us the reasons why we shouldn't obey those promptings. So we don't.

Let me tell you something: If you insist on being ruled by your natural reasoning and human intellect, the Spirit of God won't be able to get much over to you. Even when He does, you will talk yourself out of it because, quite often, what God tells you to do will not make sense to your mind. His thoughts are so much higher than ours. (See Isaiah 55:8–9.)

Once, when I first began learning to hear the voice of God, I was standing on the front row during the altar call at one of Ken's meetings. He had given the invitation, and quite a few people had come to the front of the auditorium. Among them was a young girl about fifteen years old. When she walked up there, I sensed an urging in my spirit: *Go up and put your arms around her and love her.*

Was that You, Lord? I asked silently. *Or was that me?* I wasn't sure, so I just stood there. Then that impression came back again. *Go up and put your arms around that girl and love her.*

Still, I wasn't sure. Then I began to think of reasons why I shouldn't do it. *I don't want to go up there in front of all those people...I've never done anything like that before...and anyway, I don't even know this girl.* That's the danger of not moving when the Lord tells us to move. We begin to reason, which is the worst thing we can do where walking in the spirit is concerned.

But since I had asked God to teach me how to follow Him, He didn't give up on me. As I stood there trying to remain sensitive to God, I heard Ken say, "Gloria, come up here and put your arm around this girl and just love her." Clearly, God was telling me, *Yes!* That was His prompting in my heart telling me what to do just as I had asked Him!

Later, when I thought about it, I realized it wouldn't have made much difference if I had obeyed that prompting and been wrong. It wasn't a matter of life and death; it was just a matter of being embarrassed.

That's usually how it is. God won't ask you to part the Red Sea the first day you start learning to hear His voice. He won't tell you to risk your life. He is a master teacher. He knows how to start where you are and deal with you perfectly.

But to obey Him you have to become like a little child. You have to be simple enough to just trust Him and do whatever He tells you to do. Jesus said in Matthew 18:4, "Whosoever therefore shall humble himself as this little child, the same is greatest in the kingdom of heaven." If you want to be spiritually strong, you have to stop worrying about your image. You have to stop being concerned about looking foolish and caring more about how you look to people than about how you look to God.

You must be willing to humble yourself under the mighty hand of God and do whatever He says, even if you think it will make you look silly. And you might as well know right now that some of His instructions will make you look silly to worldly people, because they don't understand God's ways.

God told Isaiah, for example, to go naked and barefoot for three years. (He really did! You can read about it in Isaiah 20. *The Amplified Bible* says that he "stripped to his loincloth" [v. 2].) Don't you know Isaiah looked strange to the people around him? But God said it was a sign and a wonder. Now I have no understanding of that, but it serves to remind me that God's ways are very different from our ways.

I can tell you, I didn't go very far in following the Holy Spirit until I said, "Lord, I don't care what I look like to others. If You tell me to do something, I'll do it."

Once you make that decision, obeying God will become much simpler. When you decide you would rather look ridiculous than risk being disobedient, you're on the verge of an enormous breakthrough, because as you follow His promptings, they grow clearer in your spirit. Knowing what God says in His Word will help you to determine whether the thought or prompting was from God. The Holy Spirit will never tell you to do anything that disagrees with the written Word.

Stop Wishing and Start Expecting

If you're like me, once you begin to identify the leading of the Spirit, you will realize you've heard from God in many instances when you didn't even know it. You obeyed the prompting of the Spirit, but because you were expecting something stronger and bolder, you didn't recognize that prompting or unction as a leading from God.

It will probably dawn on you that God has been speaking to you since the day you were born again. He wasn't speaking to you in a way that you could hear with your natural ears. He was speaking to you by enlightening your spirit.

I remember one time in particular when God was very clearly leading me, but I had no idea He was doing it. It was years ago when Ken and I were preaching in Hawaii. The morning we were scheduled to leave, I woke up with a strong desire for a macadamia nut waffle. (The Holy Spirit would never use a macadamia nut waffle to lead Ken, because he doesn't eat things like that. I do, however, and it worked very well for me.)

Of course, I didn't know that hunger was of the Lord. I just thought, *A waffle sounds like a great idea!* So I rushed around and told Ken and the children that I would go down to the restaurant and find a table. They could meet me there, and we would eat breakfast before we headed for the airport.

When I entered the restaurant, there were two lines: one was for people who wanted tables outside and the other was for people who wanted to eat inside. I always like to eat outside, but that day I thought, *Well, we'll just eat inside today because we're in a hurry and that line is shorter.*

Then an odd thing happened. Just when it was my turn to be seated, a man stepped right in front of me and took the table that should have been mine. When the hostess came back for me, she led me to a table that was all the way in the back of this large restaurant. At first, I sat down on one side of the table. Then, because I wanted to be able to see Ken and the children when they came in, I moved to the other side of the table.

The chair I chose was right next to a lady who was eating

breakfast. I couldn't have been any closer to her unless I sat in her lap. She was right beside me.

As I sat down, she burst into tears. Then she spoke to me, put something in my hand and said, "The Lord told me yesterday to give you this ring."

When I saw her tears, I thought perhaps she really didn't want to give it. So I suggested she wait a while and pray about it some more.

"Oh, no!" she said. "I'm not crying because I don't want you to have it. I'm crying because I'm happy. You see, I'm new at learning to hear from God, and yesterday I thought the Lord told me to give this ring to you. I said, 'Lord, if it's really You telling me this, cause Gloria to sit next to me at breakfast in the morning.'"

Obviously the Lord had been leading me through all the choices I had made that morning because I not only sat next to her—I nearly sat on top of her.

That ring was such a blessing to me! It was very unusual. It was a diamond and emerald ring with a setting that constantly spun around and around. During that particular meeting, I had received the revelation of the hundredfold return coming to us in this life, and every time I looked at that ring, it reminded me that my hundredfold return was constantly working, coming to me in this life. (See Mark 10:30.)

If you are sitting there right now wishing things like that would happen to you, stop wishing and start expecting. Then step out and obey the promptings you receive. (I had given a diamond ring away just a few days before because I was prompted to do it.)

Don't be afraid of making a mistake. You have the protection of knowing that the Holy Spirit will never lead you contrary to God's written Word. So don't let fear hold you back anymore. Keep your spirit in communion with the Holy Spirit, and begin to trust in His ability to lead and guide you.

He can't do anything for you until you trust Him. Just as Jesus couldn't fulfill His ministry as Savior in your life until you trusted Him to save you, the Holy Spirit can't fulfill His role as Comforter, Standby, Helper and Teacher in your life until you depend on Him to do those things. He is waiting on you!

Don't keep Him waiting any longer. Develop a lifestyle of hearing from the Spirit of God by maintaining your fellowship with Him and daring to believe He will lead you. Yes, even you!

CHAPTER 16

Principles of Divine Direction

The Holy Spirit speaks to us and gives us direction through God's Word, which is where we find wisdom and understanding about conducting our lives wisely, living in peace and joy, and walking in health and prosperity. We get divine direction from the Word as the Holy Spirit leads us to various scriptures and reveals them to us.

When I first started learning about God's Word, I didn't know what I know now about being taught by the Holy Spirit. But one day I was studying Proverbs in *The Amplified Bible,* and I came across Proverbs 16:3. I knew He had led me to one of those priceless treasures of the Word!

In the years since then, the truth the Holy Spirit revealed in that scripture has helped me in my walk with God again and again. So we're going to "camp" on this verse for a while as we explore the principles of divine direction found in this chapter and throughout the Word of God.

Roll Your Works on the Lord

When I first discovered Proverbs 16:3, I was very excited to find such a wonderful key to receiving God's direction in my life! This is what it says in *The Amplified Bible:* "Roll your works upon the Lord [commit and trust them wholly to Him; He will cause your thoughts to become agreeable to His will, and] so shall your plans be established and succeed."

At that time, I didn't have much confidence in my ability to make wise decisions. God was just beginning to teach me about listening to my heart. So I took this scripture and began to use it in my life and expect God to give me His thoughts. It worked for me!

"Roll your works upon the Lord." Now, that's a crucial first step. The rest of the verse will never happen if you don't do that first. You have to *wholly* commit and trust them to Him. You have to maintain an attitude of trust in order to walk in this verse. First Peter 5:7 says, "Casting all your care upon him; for he careth for you." You can't be worried or fearful. After you roll all your care over on Him, expect your thoughts to become agreeable to His will. God will reveal His thoughts to you concerning the matter, and as you agree with Him and obey, your plans will be established and successful. Of course, this won't work if you aren't living for God. You can't live a godless life and still expect your thoughts to become agreeable to God's thoughts. But when you seek after God, walking in all the light you have and spending time in His Word, you can expect God to give you His thoughts. That's how He communicates with us in our walk with Him.

In other words, as we seek God and give Him place in our

thoughts, He puts His thoughts on the inside of us. Then His thoughts rise from our spirit (heart) into our mind.

You may be unsure whether the thoughts you are thinking are yours or His. But if you'll pay attention to your heart, something deep down inside of you will let you know His thoughts from yours. You'll just know.

For example, if you're about to embark in a direction that isn't agreeable to God's will, you'll sense a scratching, an uneasiness, a lack of peace down in your spirit. When you sense that uneasiness, stop and find out why it's there. The Holy Spirit is trying to tell you something. Take time and listen.

That's the way I walk through life. I won't make a major decision if I have uneasiness concerning God's will on the matter. Many times that makes me slower than others in getting something done, but it's worth it.

On the issues of life, I want peace in my heart. And if the matter is critical or involves something that could change the course of my life, I want more than peace. I want positive assurance to confirm the way He wants me to go.

But in most of my everyday life, I follow that sense of peace in my heart. I expect God to make my thoughts agreeable to His will. I expect Him to give me direction.

In Acts 15:28 James says, "For it seemed good to the Holy Ghost, and to us...." Sometimes I go by what seems good to me and what I believe seems good to the Lord. In other words, if I have peace about something, it seems good to go in that direction. It is difficult to articulate, but if you are walking in love and following God with your whole heart, you will know.

Even when we make a mistake, if our heart is right, God will reconcile things for us.

Let Peace Rule in Your Life

About the time I first discovered Proverbs 16:3, I found another scripture that goes along with it. Both of these verses together taught me how to follow the Lord's leading even before I really understood what I was doing.

The second scripture I found that helped me was Colossians 3:15 (*The Amplified Bible*): "And let the peace (soul harmony which comes) from Christ rule (act as umpire continually) in your hearts [deciding and settling with finality all questions that arise in your minds]."

God's peace is to continually act as an umpire in your heart and mind! Suppose you are considering taking a certain direction and you don't have peace about it. You just aren't sure what God's will is on the matter.

Well, if you don't have peace about the step you're about to take, *don't do it*. Spend time praying about it. (This is when praying in the spirit really helps. When you don't know, you need to be able to let the Holy Spirit give you utterance.) Hold it before the Lord until you know the right thing to do. Always follow peace.

Now, that sense of peace isn't a strong, tangible feeling. It's something you have to watch and listen for.

As I mentioned earlier, sometimes we describe the leading of the Holy Spirit in our hearts as an *unction* or an *inner witness*. We have to look inside our spirit and see what the Spirit of God is telling us to do.

Before I understood much about the inward witness, I let the peace of God be the umpire in my heart. And even today, when I have peace about a decision, I have a tendency to go ahead and do it. But if I don't have peace about it, I'll hold off and wait until I know for sure what to do.

Sometimes I probably wait too long, but I have discovered over the years that God isn't in a hurry; therefore, I shouldn't be in a hurry either. (Best of all, I stay out of a lot of trouble by this method of making decisions!)

God Creates His Desires in You

Rolling your works on the Lord is a very important element of following Him. As you do that, He causes your thoughts to become agreeable to His will. This principle agrees with Proverbs 3:6, which says, "In all thy ways acknowledge him, and he shall direct thy paths."

When you begin to order your life according to the Word of God, you'll find that most of what God has laid out for you to do are things that you desire to do. Actually, God creates the desire in you: "It is God who is all the while effectually at work in you [energizing and creating in you the power and desire], both to will and to work for His good pleasure and satisfaction and delight" (Philippians 2:13, AMP).

So when you walk with God, your desires will normally flow *with,* not *against,* His desires. He will speak a thought into your heart, and it will be as if He turned His light on the situation. You'll think, *Wow! I never looked at it like that. Why didn't I think of that before? This is the answer!*

Well, that's God giving you His thoughts concerning that matter. Most of the time, God's thoughts that come up from your spirit to your mind are pleasant. You'll just know they are right. You'll say, "That sounds good to me. I see that."

Maintain a Grateful Heart

The last part of Colossians 3:15 (AMP) is also a very important key to flowing with God: "And be thankful (appreciative), [giving praise to God always]."

You know, it's hard to hear what God is saying in your spirit if you let little things irritate you all the time. When God's peace isn't ruling in your life, you're always stirred up about some outside circumstance. That's why it's so difficult to hear what is in your spirit.

But when you maintain a thankful, grateful heart, it's so much easier to hear what the Holy Spirit is saying down in your spirit. You get up in the morning, and you're grateful for the new day. You aren't mad at God because He didn't do more for you yesterday. You are grateful for what He *has* done.

God has already done so much for us. If He never did another thing, we'd still be grateful to Him for the rest of our lives. Yet He never stops blessing us. That's why it's so important to maintain a grateful heart, focusing on all He does for us rather than on the little frustrations of life.

So if you have a tendency to let everything irritate you, it's time to overcome that tendency. I guarantee you, this world isn't perfect. And if you expect your days to flow perfectly with no bumps along the way, you'll always be frustrated and disappointed.

There will always be people in this world who try to stir you up to anger or don't treat you right. But you just need to walk right through all the irritations of life without letting them steal your peace. Learn to exercise your faith by rolling your care over on Him. Let's look at 1 Peter 5:6–9 in *The Amplified Bible:*

> *Therefore humble yourselves [demote, lower yourselves in your own estimation] under the mighty hand of God, that in due time He may exalt you, casting the whole of your care [all your anxieties, all your worries, all your concerns, once and for all] on Him, for He cares for you affectionately and cares about you watchfully. Be well balanced (temperate, sober of mind), be vigilant and cautious at all times; for that enemy of yours, the devil, roams around like a lion roaring [in fierce hunger], seeking someone to seize upon and devour. Withstand him; be firm in faith [against his onset— rooted, established, strong, immovable, and determined], knowing that the same (identical) sufferings are appointed to your brotherhood (the whole body of Christians) throughout the world.*

Rolling your care over on the Lord is an important strategy of walking in faith. You are resisting doubt and fear and at the same time placing yourself in a position of faith. Keep yourself there by refusing to allow worry or fear to have a place in your life.

I'm telling you, *fight to keep your peace.* That peace is so important to your well-being. Living in peace not only makes it easier to hear from God, but it keeps your body healthier.

Just let this be a challenge to you: Don't let the devil use people or irritations to steal your peace and joy. Don't let him fill your mind with unbelief, doubt, fear and worry. Learn to live from the inside out! Make it your goal that *nothing* will keep you from discerning the direction of God in your life. Let peace rule, no matter what is going on around you.

Stop Worrying

Worry is one of the biggest thieves of peace there is. It becomes a major problem when you fail to roll your works on the Lord.

I remember when I learned to quit worrying and to commit all my ways to the Lord. I had grown up in a family that didn't know it was possible *not* to worry. Some members of my family were expert worriers!

For several years after I was born again, I didn't have any teaching in the Word. But I had *The Amplified Bible,* so two friends and I would meet at least once a week to read it together.

Whenever we received a little light on a scripture, we'd act on it—and it would work for us! Actually, the principles we learned began to work in our lives before we ever comprehended how those principles fit into the whole plan of God.

Then I began to see that I couldn't have faith and worry at the same time, so I decided to quit worrying. I had to quit one minute at a time because worry was such a habit with me. Actually, I used to think if I didn't worry, I wasn't being responsible.

So every time a worried thought came to me, I would overcome it with the Word of God. I would push the thought away and quote from the Word. I just continued to do that minute by minute until eventually worry stopped being a habit with me. (That had to be the Holy Spirit prompting me to do that. I didn't know enough to figure it out on my own!)

Maybe worry isn't your problem. Perhaps your habit is strife. For instance, do you get all stirred up for the rest of the day when someone says something the least bit unkind to you?

Well, you can get rid of strife the same way I got rid of worry. If you have to, just start dealing with it a moment at a time. If you have to quote the Word fifteen times every thirty minutes to overcome strife, then do it. Every time strife tries to attach itself to you, resist it and say, "I'm walking in the peace of God!" You'll be surprised at how much more pleasant your life will be.

You see, you'll always have the opportunity for worry and strife. You just have to make the decision to stay in peace no matter what. It's a vital step in learning to hear from God.

The Bible says where there is envy and strife, there is confusion and every evil work. So strife is one of the devil's most valuable tools. Read all of James 3 to gain valuable understanding.

Walk in What You Already Know

Walking in the fear of God is also a vital principle in receiving direction from the Lord. Proverbs 16:6 (AMP) says, "By the reverent, worshipful fear of the Lord men depart from and avoid evil."

You see, the reason you decide to overcome worry or strife or anything else that blocks your communication with God is that you have more reverence for God than you do for your own selfish desires. When you walk in the fear of God and you know the right thing to do, you will do what's right because you want to honor God.

Most believers are troubled *not* by the fact that they don't know the right thing to do, but because they aren't doing what they know to do.

Yes, there's a lot we *don't* know. But if we'd just do what we know to do, we'd be living on a much higher spiritual level today in our walk with God.

So do what you know to do to receive direction from the Lord. He wants to make your thoughts agreeable to His will, but that process just doesn't happen automatically. Roll your works upon Him. Rid yourself of anything that keeps you from hearing His voice. Walk in the fear of God, letting peace rule as umpire in your heart.

God has given you these principles of divine direction for a reason. He wants to help guide you not only through your daily life, but to your appointed destiny in Him!

Commit every situation you are facing today to the Lord once and for all and refuse to take it back. Trust Him with your life.

CHAPTER 17

Guard Your Heart

Everything in your life begins in your heart. Your future is literally stored up in your heart. As Jesus said, "A good man out of the good treasure of the heart bringeth forth good things: and an evil man out of the evil treasure bringeth forth evil things" (Matthew 12:35).

What you will have in your life tomorrow will be determined by what is in your heart today. If you allow your heart to be filled with the cares and anxieties of life, to be crowded with worries and thoughts of this natural world, then your future will be marked, not by the supernatural blessings of God, but by the sickness, poverty and calamity this world brings.

If, on the other hand, you fill your heart with the Word of God and the things of God, fellowshiping with Him each day and feasting your heart on His promises and His presence, then your future will be one of joy and prosperity, healing and health. Instead of chasing after the blessings of God, you will find they are chasing you and overtaking you at every turn!

How do you keep your heart in such a state of divine fullness? By doing what we've talked about again and again in this book—

by spending time with the Lord every single day and by making that time with Him your number one priority.

Notice I said your *number one* priority. As precious as your family is, it is not the most important thing in your life. (Your family will benefit immensely from this commitment.) Your career is not the most important thing. Spending time with God is the most important thing, and once you realize that, you will do whatever you have to do to find that time. You will wake up earlier in the morning or go to bed later at night. You will change jobs if necessary. You'll eliminate things from your life that steal your time away.

You'll never regret it either, because if you keep that union with the Lord as your number one priority, He will take care of everything else.

"But Gloria," you might say, "that sounds so hard!"

If it were easy, everybody would be doing it. It is difficult in that it takes continual commitment, but it is easy in that it allows the Spirit of God to manifest the blessing of God in every area of your life. It allows God's supernatural power to have free course. There is no other way. There is no substitute. There's nothing else that will replace time and attention given to the Lord. That is the only thing that will make everything else work. The Scripture says:

> *Be not deceived; God is not mocked: for whatsoever a man soweth, that shall he also reap. For he that soweth to his flesh shall of the flesh reap corruption; but he that soweth to the Spirit shall of the Spirit reap life everlasting. And let us not be weary in well doing: for in due season we shall reap, if we faint not.* (Galatians 6:7–9)

You might be able to fool yourself into thinking you can prosper by cutting down on your time with God and increasing your time at work, but you can't fool God. You cannot avoid His principles. You can't plant one thing in your heart and reap another. Don't be deceived. You can't fill your heart and time and affections with the natural things of this world and have strong faith in the time of trouble.

It doesn't matter if you've been in the ministry fifty years and have the gifts of the Spirit operating through you in mighty ways. If you don't spend time in the Word and fellowshiping with the Spirit of God, spiritually you will come up short. You won't have supernatural power in your life when you need it.

That may sound like bad news to some, but really it's good news! Because the law of sowing and reaping always works, you will never sow to the spirit and come up empty-handed. If you sow to the spirit, you are sure to reap life from the spirit. You will reap wisdom and strength and provision. You will enjoy a continual flow of all that God has and is. You will be constantly supplied with everything that pertains to life and godliness. (See 2 Peter 1:3.)

What Choice Are You Making Today?

Since our future is stored up in our hearts and every single believer has the ability to keep his own heart full of the Word and the Spirit of God, we all have the same opportunity to be blessed in every way. God is no respecter of persons. God has said to us, just as He said to Israel:

I call heaven and earth to record this day against you, that I have set before you life and death, blessing and cursing: therefore choose life, that both thou and thy seed may live. (Deuteronomy 30:19)

Your future is not thrust upon you without your consent. You choose it every day by giving God first place in your life or by putting the natural things of the world first place. You choose it by planting the seeds of God's Word in your heart each day or by entertaining the doubts and fears of the world, the flesh and the devil.

I said it before and I'll say it again because I want you to remember it: Everything you receive from God begins in your heart. That's where you are born again. That is where the Holy Spirit lives. That's where the Word is deposited. Everything supernatural that you receive comes out of your heart!

Some people assume that because they have spent days or even years studying the Word of God and know what it says, they will enjoy a harvest of God's blessing. But remember this: It is the choice you make today—not the choice you made yesterday or last month or last year—that will determine your tomorrow. For yesterday's seed, if it is not watered today by your fellowship with God, will be overcome by weeds. The cares of this world, the deceitfulness of riches and the lusts of other things entering in will choke the Word and make it unfruitful. (See Mark 4:19.)

Every day we must obey the instructions in Proverbs 4:20–23:

My son, attend to my words; incline thine ear unto my sayings. Let them not depart from thine eyes; keep them in the midst of thine heart. For they are life unto those that find them, and health to all their flesh. Keep thy heart with all diligence; for out of it are the issues of life.

You deposit the Word in your heart by keeping it in front of your eyes and going into your ears. God has blessed this generation with more ways to do this than any other generation has ever enjoyed. We not only have books, but we have multiple forms of audio and video resources as well as Christian television broadcasts and the Internet. We also have the anointed Word being preached in churches and conventions all over the world.

If we don't keep God's Word in our eyes and ears, it's our own fault!

Even though we have all these avenues available to us, we still have to make a quality decision to be diligent. A quality decision is one from which there is no turning back. To be diligent means you don't let anything else interfere with what you have determined to do. You cannot be diligent and lazy at the same time.

Noah Webster's 1828 *American Dictionary of the English Language* says *diligent* means "steady application to business; constant in effort or exertion to accomplish what is undertaken; industrious; not idle or negligent."[10] To successfully keep our hearts and walk in victory in this life, we have to be that way about the time we spend with God and His Word.

If we will diligently apply ourselves to keeping our hearts by staying in daily contact with God through the Word and through prayer, His supernatural power will continually flow out of our innermost beings. The forces of divine life—forces such as faith, love, joy, patience and the other fruit of the spirit—will constantly spring forth from our hearts to empower us and enable us to overcome in every area of life.

Years ago, the Spirit of God gave me an unforgettable illustration of that truth. I was preparing to teach a healing service in the Philippines, and I was meditating on that very scripture in Proverbs 4:23: "Keep and guard your heart with all vigilance and above all that you guard, for out of it flow the springs of life" (AMP).

As I thought about that verse, I looked out the window and saw the fountain in front of my hotel. The water in it was shooting up into the air with great force.

As I watched it, the Lord drew my attention to the fact that as long as there was an outflow of water from that fountain, no trash could remain in it. Even if it were just barely flowing over the top, it would wash away all debris. If you turn the water up high, the force of it would be so strong that nothing could even get close to the mouth of it.

That's the way our heart is. As long as we keep an overflow and as long as we have the forces of God coming out of it, Satan's junk will be forced out of our lives and things will be well with us. But we don't have to settle for just a little overflow. We can turn those forces up high. We can have a gusher of God's power, joy, love and wisdom issuing forth from within us.

If we want to, we can be so full of God and so full of the Word and time with Him, that sickness and disease can't even get close to our bodies. We can be flowing so strongly with God's divine life that it becomes as difficult for us to get sick as it once was for us to get healed. If we will learn to live in constant contact with God, we can experience the divine health that John G. Lake described. We can live "day by day and hour by hour in touch with God so that the life of God flows into the body, just as the life of God flows into the mind or flows into the spirit."[11]

You're Building for Eternity

When you think of what's available to us in God, it is not amazing that we find time to spend with Him, but that we find time to do anything else! With all He has to offer, it would seem we would be willing to make any sacrifice to spend time with Him. Look at what we would miss. Look at what we would give up: sickness, fear, poverty, sin and unbelief!

But all too often, Christians don't think that way. They're like the people God spoke to in Jeremiah 2:13, saying, "For my people have committed two evils; they have forsaken me the fountain of living waters, and hewed them out cisterns, broken cisterns, that can hold no water."

Instead of seeking God—the fountain of prosperity—many believers spend all their time trying to secure high-paying jobs or building big businesses. Instead of partaking of the fountain of healing, they rush to the doctor's office and spend hours there because they are too busy with the natural affairs of life to make daily contact with God.

If you don't spend time every day drinking from the fountain of living waters, I don't care how spiritual you may have been in the past, when Satan comes to defeat you, you won't put your foot on his head like you should. Your faith won't be as strong and aggressive as it should be. You'll put up with the devil's garbage.

You might say a little prayer, but it won't have any power because you haven't been spending time with God.

You need to continue partaking of the living waters. You need to maintain an overflow in your heart. You don't always have time to find your Bible in the time of danger or crisis. When you come up against something unexpected, whatever you've been depositing in your heart will come out. You have to stay ready all the time. You don't want to face a life-or-death situation and find yourself without an overflow—and have fear and unbelief come out of your mouth instead of faith.

If you find yourself in that spot, it won't be God's responsibility. It will be your own responsibility. You have a choice. You can drink from Him—the fountain of living waters—or you can forsake Him for the concerns and entertainments of this natural world.

Am I saying you should never spend any time on natural things? Of course not. We live in natural bodies and have natural duties we must perform. There are times when it's good to relax and enjoy some recreation. God expects and desires that we enjoy life. He enjoys life, and His desire for us is the same. When we put Him first, we live in joy. We get more out of natural life than we ever have before, because God manifests Himself in everything we do. In His presence is fullness of joy. (See Psalm 16:11.) Romans 8:6 says "to be spiritually minded is life and peace." That's the most enjoyment possible in this life! But always remember this: Every moment you spend on natural things is lost forever. When it's gone, it's gone, and you have nothing lasting to show for it.

The time you spend with God, however, is time spent building for eternity. When it's over, it's not over. Every moment spent with

God further opens the door to His wonderful blessings and everlasting rewards.

You are building for eternity right now. The minutes and hours and days of your life are the only blocks you have with which to build. So don't waste them. Use them wisely. Let your spirit be your guide. In other words, listen to your heart. For in the end, it is only the time you have given to God that will count.

CHAPTER 18

Pressing In—It's Worth It All

When you guard your heart by choosing to abide in God's Word and to obey the wise counsel of the Holy Spirit, that means you want to be victorious over every challenge in life. You want to be a winner! But what does it take to be a winner? Everyone wants to know the answer to that question! We all want to win. But when it comes right down to it, few of us are willing to pay the price.

One day I heard an Olympic athlete describe how hard she had worked for the opportunity to compete in the Olympic Games. She was telling what it took for her to win the gold medal.

Olympic athletes don't just wake up one morning and say, "Hey! I think I'll be in the Olympics today." They train for years to get there. Some of them train most of their lives.

They get out of bed every morning to run. They run in the cold. They run in the rain. They run no matter what—whether they want to or not. This woman said there were times when she pushed herself so hard she became physically ill. But even then, she refused to stop running.

That woman was determined to win.

She had decided years earlier to go for a gold medal—no matter what the cost. She was stretching and straining to win it, pushing forward with the kind of force that moves every obstacle out of the way.

That kind of force is what it takes to be a winner—not just physically but spiritually. Jesus said this in Matthew 11:12, "And from the days of John the Baptist until now the kingdom of heaven suffereth violence, and the violent take it by force."

In this verse, Jesus wasn't talking about going to heaven. He was talking about taking hold of the kingdom of God on this earth—actually possessing the promised blessings like healing, prosperity and peace.

You can have those kingdom blessings now. But it's not easy— you have to take them by force.

Press In

The fact is, if you want to lay hold of the authority of God and walk in the supernatural, you can't do it from your easy chair. You have to press in. Jesus said, "The law and the prophets were until John: since that time the kingdom of God is preached, and every man presseth into it" (Luke 16:16). Paul wrote, "...I press on to lay hold of (grasp) and make my own, that for which Christ Jesus (the Messiah) has laid hold of me and made me His own" (Philippians 3:12, AMP).

Press in. That's as important a concept for us today as it was in Moses' time. Moses pressed in the Spirit. He wanted to see God's glory. I'm that way too. I'd want to see God's glory even if I knew I wouldn't live through it.

That heart cry to know God keeps us pressing in to lay hold of more of His kingdom each day of our lives. It pushes us toward the goal of knowing Jesus and finishing the race God has set before us. If you want to go on with God like Moses and Paul did, then that desire must become the cry of your heart. Paul's heart cry to know the Lord made him determined not to quit. He was determined to press on until he laid hold of every task the Lord had for him. One day in the midst of persecuting the Church, Paul was laid hold of by Jesus. The *King James Version* of the Bible says he was "apprehended" by Jesus. From the time he was saved until the time he went to be with the Lord, Paul was committed to fulfill the calling for which he was apprehended. He would not quit early.

Finish Your Race

Like Paul's race, there's also a race marked out for you. God charted that course and only you can run it. Only by pressing in to win your race will you see the fullness of God's provision in your life.

And let me add: God didn't choose you for that race based on your ability, intellect or anything you could do in the natural. He planned to empower you with *His* ability to do the job He prepared for you. It's in the weakness of your natural ability that He can show Himself strong. Don't be deceived into thinking someone else can run your race. No one can run another person's race.

If we knew the races that were marked out for everyone ahead of time, we'd probably choose different people to run them. We would think, *I won't choose that person—they'll never make it!*

Let me tell you how God picks people for their tasks: He looks at the heart. He doesn't usually choose people from the greatest universities. It's difficult for Him to use those who think they can handle situations in their own wisdom and strength.

I want to tell you something that will take a lot of pressure off you and will release faith action: Whatever your qualifications, *the race you have been chosen to run is impossible to finish on your own.* God plans so big you couldn't possibly do it in your own strength and intelligence. It takes faith in Him to finish the race.

It took a lot of pressure off me when I realized God never intended for us to know how to do what He tells us to do. He never intended for Ken or me to know how to go on television. He intended to do it through us. *He* knows how! We just have to do what we're told.

Our part is to maintain our fellowship with Him. His part is to do the work through us. When you're in God, you're over your head all the time. Get used to it and keep on pressing in.

No Time to Hesitate

If there were ever a generation that needed to press in to the things of God, it's our generation. I believe we are living in the last days. I believe Jesus is coming soon and that helps me to keep my life focused on Him.

In recent times, the Church has not given enough attention to Jesus' soon return. The fact that He could come at any moment ought to be foremost in our hearts. We ought to preach it to people and share it.

The Scripture says our hope of His return purifies us. (See 1 John 3:3.) People wouldn't pour so much energy into material-istic things if they thought Jesus was coming back in less than a decade. They wouldn't be as carnal. They'd be pressing in to the things of the Spirit and storing up heavenly rewards.

Now is our opportunity to do that! Our rewards, our rank, even our responsibilities in heaven will be determined by what we do here on earth. For a few brief years here, we have the opportunity to influence people around us—to let the character of the Lord Jesus Christ and the love of God flow out through us and reveal God to the world.

Soon that opportunity will be gone. In the meantime, it's worth living for...it's worth dying for...it's worth whatever sacrifices we have to make.

Go Ahead, Assert Yourself!

How do you get the kind of spiritual aggressiveness, the urgency it takes to lay hold of that opportunity?

First, you must determine your focus and spend time with God. The Apostle Paul said, "*[For my determined purpose is] that I may know Him* [that I may progressively become more deeply and intimately acquainted with Him]..." (Philippians 3:10, AMP).

Notice Paul didn't say, "One of my purposes is...." He said very specifically, "My *determined* purpose is...." I can promise you this: You won't be spiritually aggressive unless you determine to be. You'll let "...the cares of this world, and the deceitfulness of riches, and the lusts of other things" get in your way (Mark 4:19).

I need to warn you, that determination to spend time with God will run headlong into a busy life. To stay on course, you will have to bring your flesh under the rule of your spirit and be willing to simplify your life.

Seizing the kingdom isn't easy. God doesn't say it will be easy, but He does say it will be worth it.

These times demand that you take time to be with the Lord, that you put your flesh down and stir your faith up.

Once you have made the quality decision to know God—to become more deeply and intimately acquainted with Him—your second step is to spend time with Him. That's always the bottom line, isn't it? Whenever we start pressing in, desiring to win more victories in the spirit, desiring more power, we're always directed back to that precious time with Him.

Look again at what Paul said, "[For my determined purpose is] that I may know Him...and that I may in that same way come to know the power outflowing from His resurrection..." (Philippians 3:10, AMP).

Think about it. If you spend an hour with God every day, that's 365 hours a year. Don't you think coming into His presence for an hour every day will do something for your life? Even if you just spent fifteen minutes a day, that would be ninety hours a year of prayer and time with Him. Follow your own heart. But see to it that you give the Father time to impart His strength into you.

Do you want Jesus' resurrection power to flow in your life? Then get to know Him! The more you fellowship with Him, the more you're going to look like Him, act like Him and talk like Him.

That's not surprising, really. It's a fact of life. When you spend time around strong people, you begin to take on their way of talking, thinking and even their mannerisms. When you spend time with Jesus, you'll do exactly the same thing.

So, if you spend your time watching secular television and filling your mind with the world's news, what do you think will happen? You'll end up being like the world and living in fear instead of faith.

What you give your attention to is what will be on the inside of you. And what's inside you will determine the outcome of your situation. Your future is stored up in your heart. Jesus said in Matthew 12:34–35, "You brood of vipers, how can you who are evil say anything good? For out of the overflow of the heart the mouth speaks. The good man brings good things out of the good stored up in him, and the evil man brings evil things out of the evil stored up in him" (NIV).

Press Toward the Mark

Once your focus and your fellowship are in place, press. To *press* means "to act with steady force or weight; to be insistent about; to exert pressure." It means "to go forward with energetic or determined effort."

Paul said, "I press toward the mark for the prize of the high calling of God in Christ Jesus" (Philippians 3:14).

To be a winner, you press. You press in to what God has called you to do. You don't float into it. You press forward by faith, believing the Word of God regardless of what you see with your natural eyes or hear with your natural ears.

No matter where you are today in your spiritual growth, you won't progress without pressing. Remember what I said about those Olympic athletes? They know what it means to press toward a goal. They know what it means to put everything else aside. They know what it means to win the prize.

If natural people with natural discipline and desire to reach a goal can do that, certainly you and I can do it in the Spirit! We can do it with the power of the Holy Spirit in us and the Word of God in our hearts and in our mouths. We can press until we finish the race God has called us to run.

Remember, the natural world will always tell you that you can't do it—it's too big for you. You're too foolish. You're too weak. But God just says, *Do it, and I'll make up the difference.*

Stretch Toward the Finish Line

That means we stretch forward to the things in front of us. We bear down on the goal.

Paul was so intensely focused on pursuing the prize of his call in Christ that he would not allow himself to look anywhere but toward the goal. He ran, "forgetting those things which are behind, and reaching forth unto those things which are before..." (Philippians 3:13).

Paul never stopped stretching. When he was imprisoned, he wrote most of the New Testament. How was he able to do this? Look at Acts 20:22–24 (emphasis mine):

And now, behold, I go bound in the spirit unto Jerusalem, not knowing the things that shall befall me there: save that the Holy Ghost witnesseth in every city, saying that bonds and afflictions abide me. But none of these things move me, neither count I my life dear unto myself, so that I might finish my course with joy, and the ministry, which I have received of the Lord Jesus, to testify the gospel of the grace of God.

Paul could stretch toward the goal without distraction because he didn't count his life dear to himself. He had found something worth giving his life for. One day while I was reading this scripture the Lord impressed me, *Gloria, this is the key to your success spiritually. If you count your life dear unto yourself, you won't finish your race.*

Counting your life dear to yourself means that you've let the distractions of the age get hold of you. You concentrate on what *you* want to have and what *you* want to do—*your* happiness.

Jesus said if we would lose our lives for His sake, we would find them. That's life worth living. There's no peace in living like the world and going after things. But seek Him first and His righteousness, and all the other things will come to you (Matthew 6:33).

The Joy of Winning

Paul knew where to look for his joy. He said he would "finish [his] course with joy." He was going to complete the ministry to which he had been called. He did not focus on his own life—his personal desires. He was going to finish his race, and when he crossed the line, there was going to be a smile on his face.

He intended not only to finish but to do it with joy. I like that. I, too, am not only going to finish my race and win, but I'm going to enjoy it!

Do you see that we're not talking about a race in which we drag up to the finish line depressed and despondent? We are talking about a race God intends for us to finish with joy.

Don't let the natural realm determine your level of courage or disappointment. The life of spirit beings is not sustained in the natural. A lot of our troubles are caused because our desires are incorrectly focused. Peace and joy, however, belong to those who keep their hearts full of God. So look in the right places for your joy.

Don't get distracted by anything—even legitimate things. If they have preeminence in your life, they are not right for you. One day each of us will stand before God. I personally don't think I will live out my natural life on earth. I expect Jesus to come before that happens, but one way or the other, I will stand before Him. When I do, nothing will matter except that I finished my course.

Give It All You've Got

Don't misunderstand me. God has blessed Ken and me. We're not doing without anything. We're blessed and prosperous, but the desire and motivation of our hearts is to please God. It is to walk in what we are called to do and to finish our course. We feel it's worth giving our lives in order to obtain.

You see, according to 1 Corinthians 9:24, there is a prize that all who run may obtain. But the flesh must be brought into subjection in order to win that prize:

> *Every man that striveth for the mastery is temperate in all things. Now they do it to obtain a corruptible crown; but we an incorruptible. I therefore so run, not as uncertainly; so fight I, not as one that beateth the air: But I keep under my body, and bring it into subjection: lest that by any means, when I have preached to others, I myself should be a castaway.* (1 Corinthians 9:25–27)

One translation says, "I reduce to slavery my body." We can't let our bodies rule us in this hour. We must walk in the spirit. We must crucify the flesh.

The things we turn down or accept determine the manifestation of the power of God in our lives. God's glory belongs to those who do not live after the flesh and who are no longer dominated by their bodies.

Before this age comes to a close, God will have a glorious Church—a people who refuse to live according to the dictates of the flesh or to be dominated by their bodies. He will have a Church that walks in His manifest glory.

Will You Pay the Price?

Here's the question: Do you and I want to be a part of that Church badly enough to run the race? Do we want it enough to pray and spend time in the Word instead of doing other things we could be doing—even good things?

I am one of those who love His appearing. I am believing for the Church to rise up and press in the spirit to get the things done that we need to do.

God is on a timetable. He's never late. The Church will be ready and we will do what we're called to do.

Individuals may fall out of the race. You and I could fall out if we don't do the right things—if we don't do the things we know to do. But the Church is going to finish the race, and it's going to be on time. I want to be in that group and bring God glory. For my part, I am determined to finish my course with joy.

The choice is yours; no one else can make it for you. Only you can determine in your heart, *My purpose is that I may know Him, and I'm going to press and stretch and run the race He's called me to run.*

Travel Light

Once you've made the decision to finish your race, there's one other element of spiritual aggressiveness to put into motion. Patience.

Patience doesn't sound very aggressive, does it? But it is. In Hebrews 12:1–2 Paul says, "Wherefore seeing we also are compassed about with so great a cloud of witnesses, let us lay aside every weight, and the sin which doth so easily beset us, and let us run with patience the race that is set before us, looking unto Jesus the author and finisher of our faith...."

Think about those Olympic runners. Think of them training, pushing themselves to the limit, focusing on the goal, training themselves day after day—with what? With patience! In the Greek, that word means "steady continuance."

Patience means you don't quit. You keep doing what you know to do. Sometimes you may not see results for a while. But eventually, if you keep pressing, you'll get there.

You run the race with patience and you run it unencumbered. Paul said to lay aside every weight and sin.

Weights and sin are two different things. But both of them must be removed if we are to keep running.

Weights are things that pull you down into the natural realm when you ought to be soaring in the Spirit. So let go of whatever holds you back! Press into the Spirit and run.

Sin is revealed by God's Word and the Holy Spirit's conviction.

You know when you have sinned. Confess it. Deal with it, so you can run. Lay it aside and get back on track.

Don't Get Distracted

As you lay aside weights and sin, resist distractions too. Don't allow the devil to draw your attention away. Just keep "looking unto Jesus." That's how you run this race. You can't focus on circumstances or your natural abilities. Keep your eyes on Jesus and His ability.

Peter walked on the water as long as he kept his eyes fixed on Jesus. When he began to look at the wind and the waves in the natural realm he began to sink.

Distraction can come from many directions. One of the most common tactics of the enemy is to trip you up with persecution. Don't let persecution throw you. In 2 Timothy 3:12, Paul wrote, "All that will live godly in Christ Jesus shall suffer persecution." It's just part of the package.

Don't let it stop you. Don't let it distract you.

Jesus also warned us of the distractions of this age. The deceitfulness of riches and the lusts of other things can creep in and choke the Word and make it fruitless (Mark 4:19). Near that verse in my Bible I've written the letters S-C-U-D. They stand for the phrase, "Satan Continuously Uses Distractions." He's always firing those SCUD missiles at you to discourage you and draw you off course.

Hey, he'll whisper, *have you noticed you don't have any money? Have you noticed your body is in pain? Have you heard all the ugly things people are saying about you?*

Never Give Up

How do you fight distractions like that? Just "continue thou in the things which thou hast learned and hast been assured of, knowing of whom thou hast learned them" (2 Timothy 3:14).

It won't be the great revelation you haven't received yet that will cause you defeat; it will be failing to do what you already know to do. You won't come out of the hard place when the money shows up at the bank. You'll come out when God's power, anointing and faith show up inside you.

You'll come out of your hard situation when God's Word gets so big inside you that you're not moved by what's in the bank. It may take a day or two for it to show up in the bank, but you'll get victory inside first. That never changes.

So whenever you reach a hard place, continue to do what you know and you'll make it through just fine.

You've Got What It Takes

God's Word to you is "I will be with you." When Moses asked, "Who am I to go to Pharaoh?" God's answer was, "I will be with you." After Moses' death, God told Joshua the same thing: "I will be with thee: I will not fail thee, nor forsake thee. Be strong and of a good courage..." (Joshua 1:5–6).

Even if you get into trouble by your own thinking, God will honor you if you accept correction: "...whoever heeds correction is honored" (Proverbs 13:18, NIV). Glory to God! If you press into His kingdom, stretching toward your prize, and remain correctable, He will make sure you stay headed in the right direction. He is with you and for you.

Do you wonder where your attention is? Watch your life. Watch what motivates you and what you're thinking about. Your words will follow your action. So stay alert and don't let divine things take a back seat.

Don't be dismayed. Don't lose your courage. Do what you're called to do.

You have everything it takes to be a winner—everything you need to be part of the glorious, victorious end-time army of God.

Become aggressive. Press in. Lay hold of the kingdom of God with every bit of force you can muster. That's the price you pay to win this race. But one thing is certain—the present victory as well as the eternal victory to come will be worth it all.

CHAPTER 19

If You Want a Change, Make a Change

By now, you are probably realizing that knowing God is a process of growing up spiritually. You have seen the price you must pay to win the race of the Christian life by putting God first in everything. And getting to know Him is like getting to know anyone: You must make the time to develop your relationship with Him. Whether you are a new believer or have been saved fifty years, there is always room for more of Him in your life.

If you are new to the things of God, a beginner just learning about the walk of faith, no doubt you're eager to launch into a lifestyle of spending time with God each day in prayer and the Word. That's how I was too, when I first learned what the Word of God could do.

No one had to urge me to put the Word first place. No one had to tell me to turn off the television and put down the newspaper. I totally lost interest in those things, because our lives were in such bad shape that Ken and I were desperate for God. We were in trouble. We weren't at the bottom of the barrel—we were under the barrel, and it was on top of us.

We knew that the Word of God was the only answer to our

desperate situation. So it was easy for us to sell out to it and spend time in the Word and in communion with God day and night.

You know, desperation sometimes helps. It encourages you to simplify your life. It inspires you to eliminate the unnecessary things and just go for God. But after you have walked with God for a while and things begin to be comfortable, it's easy to lose the desire you once had for the Word.

That's what happened to me. Once Ken and I paid off our debts and began enjoying the blessings of God, I began to let too much of my time be taken up by other things. They weren't sinful things; they were just things I enjoyed doing. Almost without realizing it, my appetite for the things of God began to wane. Instead of hungering more for time with Him than for anything else, I enjoyed other activities and interests more. Those activities would have been fine if I had kept them in the right place, but they occupied too much of my time and attention.

I hadn't realized it until one day in 1977 I was attending one of Kenneth Hagin's Camp Meetings and he began to prophesy. (I still keep the final words of that prophecy in my notebook today.) Part of that prophecy said to purpose in your heart that you will not be lazy; that you will not draw back, hold back or sit down; purpose in your heart that you will rise up, march forward and become on fire:

There will come a time, and we are right on the threshold of it, when further revelation concerning the power of God and concerning how to activate faith will come.

Truth has been revealed. Truth, and light, and revelation in line with God's Word come as you teach the Word, as you study the Word. But there will come further revelation concerning the power of the Lord to heal and concerning faith to operate that power that it will seem as though the Church almost immediately will rise up as a spiritual giant. And there shall be a release of power in our day, and in our age, that man has not seen before.

Oh, there is coming an hour! Gird up your loins and rejoice, Oh, ye people! There is coming an hour. There is coming a day, and it is not far off, when the truth, the full truth, the whole truth that has come here a line upon line, a precept upon precept, shall come into full revelation.

And men upon this earth shall walk, and talk, and act like God. For they'll live in the power of God motivated by His power! Motivated by His Spirit! Some will mock and laugh. And religious people, and even some who have been filled with the Spirit, will say, "They think they are 'somebody come.' They think they are God." No. They are not God. They are only children of God, agents of God, ambassadors of God who have been sent to do the works of God!

And you have only seen a little. Oh, rejoice in that which you have seen. But you have only seen a little of that which will come into fruition, into full manifestation.

The hearts of men shall rejoice and literally dance for joy. Their lips shall speak forth words of praise. You will see the lame leap like the hart and dance. You will see the blind see. You saw a small manifestation tonight, but you will see a greater manifestation. You will see those bound mentally by chains of darkness and demons loosed in a moment, for at the word of faith they must go. And you will be glad you lived in this day, in this hour, when the power of God is in manifestation.

And so those who know their God in these days shall be strong and shall do exploits. For there is an army of the Lord being raised up in this day, in this hour. Some have called them a "new breed" and speaking thusly, it is true, and it is so. Men and women, boys and girls, young men and young women who will know, and do know their rights and privileges in Christ Jesus. Who know the power of His name; who know the might of His Spirit; who know the secrets of His faith and appropriate unto themselves that which has already been given.

The Lord is raising up an army that will not run away and hide; will not run away in darkness to abide. But an army of light! An army of truth! An army of power that will go forth with His equipment and with His power and will storm the very strongholds of the devil. And the strongholds of Satan will fall flat just like the walls of Jericho fell down flat when the army of Israel, when the people of God, did what was revealed unto them by God Himself to do! And so shall it be that the Lord is raising up, and will raise up, "a spiritual army" who will go forth with His power!

In fact, many of those here tonight are a part of that army. You can be one if you so desire. Purpose in your heart that you will not be lazy; that you will not draw back, hold back, or sit down. But purpose in your heart that you will rise up, and march forward, and become on fire!

When I heard that, it dawned on me that I had let myself slip spiritually. I realized I had become lazy about the things of God. I was still spending time in the Word, but not as much as before, and I wasn't as full of zeal either. (That will always be the case. You can't be spiritually on fire without spending a sufficient amount of time with God.)

The Lord began to deal with me about it. I prayed and determined in my heart that I would change things. In order to simplify my life, I asked the Lord to show me what I should do to stir myself up.

He led me to drop certain things out of my life that were stealing my time with God. He also told me to do certain things that would stir me up and help me get back the hunger and desire I once enjoyed. A specific thing He told me was to read one of John G. Lake's sermons each day.[12] John Lake had such a spirit and revelation of dominion that every time I read one of those sermons, it opened up my heart to the power of God in a fresh way. As I began to seek God more, I became more on fire for Him and have been increasing in Him ever since.

A Tithe of Your Time

My resolve to give my time in prayer and the Word first place every day was even further strengthened in 1982 by another word from the Lord given by Kenneth E. Hagin. The Holy Spirit spoke of wading further out into the realm of the spirit, until it's so deep that you can't possibly touch the bottom. But the Spirit warned that our flesh would hold us back from that. It is only by renewing our minds that we can move into the realm of the spirit. He went on to say that if we would just give an hour or two out of every twenty-four, our lives would be changed and empowered, *all would be well,* and we would be a mighty force for God:

And in the year of 1982, there will be a year of explo-
ration in the realm of the Spirit. Yea, men and women too,
shall move into the spirit world and into the spirit realm
and into an area that they have not been before and so they
shall see and they shall know and they shall minister and
great shall be the results thereof and many hearts shall
be blessed. Some shall turn away and shake their heads in
dismay and shall say, "Oh the very idea of that." But you
see those which are earthy will grow more earthy still and
those which are spiritual will grow more spiritual still and
those who are heavenly minded will grow more heavenly
minded still and those who walk with God, for God is a
Spirit, will walk in the realm of the Spirit, will commune in
the realm of the Spirit, will see in the realm of the Spirit,
will minister in the realm of the Spirit and great shall be the
results thereof.

Some have walked out only far enough to get their feet
wet. They said, "Isn't this wonderful," and like children wad-
ing in the water they said, "This is it, this is the ultimate,
this is the finality." But oh, saith the Lords of Hosts, "That is
barely the beginning. You have only touched the realm of the
Spirit. Wade on out. Wade on out into the realm of the water
of the Spirit until it is not only knee deep and loin deep, but
until there is no way that you could possibly touch the bot-

tom, but swim on out and enjoy the fullness of that which I
have for thee, saith the Lord of Hosts."

But these things will not always come easy, for you see the
flesh will hold you back. That's the reason the Word of God
teaches you to crucify the flesh; and the (physical) man will
hold you back, and hold you into the realm of things seen
and hold you into the realm of the physical senses. That's the
reason the Bible tells you to get your mind renewed and then
you will move into the realm of the Spirit, and then there
shall be great manifestations that your heart has longed for
and the church has prayed for and the intercessors have
interceded for and the manifestation and demonstration
of the Spirit of God shall come into manifestation and into
demonstration and it shall be as common, everyday as and
just as real as everyday natural things are, for you see the
realm of the Spirit is the natural realm for the Christian who
is born of the Spirit.

But you see, you cannot walk in the natural all the time.
Oh, yes, it's necessary that you walk in the natural to a certain extent because your body is natural and your body has
natural functions and must live in that realm, but yet right
on the other hand, let your spirit have the privilege of communication with the Father of spirits. And let your spirit
move out beyond the natural.

This is the test. Light has come into the world and men
loved darkness rather than light (John 3:19).

Don't take up all your time with natural things. Some of
those things are legitimate and it's all right to take a certain
period of time there, but see to it that you give heed (watch,

listen to, pay attention) unto your spirit and you give your spirit opportunity to feed upon the Word of God and commune with the Father above and build yourself up on your most holy faith. It doesn't take a lot of time, just an hour or two out of twenty-four, just pay a tithe of your time unto Me, saith the Lord, and all will be well. Your life will be changed. It will be empowered and you will be a mighty force for God. Others will not just look at you and say, "He and she are just simply not a good example as a Christian because you see, there is so much carnality, there is so much of the flesh, there's so much of the natural." But yea, they'll see the power of the Spirit. They'll feel the love of God flowing out from you. They'll feel the rivers of the spirit of life flowing out from you, and it will bring life, and it'll bring blessing unto your own life and healing unto your own body and you will be able to minister it unto those round about you and you'll be glad, and you'll have cause for rejoicing, saith the Lord of Hosts.

That prophecy has influenced me and encouraged me tremendously throughout the years, and since I heard it, I have spent at least an hour or two alone with the Lord every day. When I began to do that, there were things in my life and family that I wanted to see changed. There were things in the lives of my children that needed to improve.

When I heard the prophet say that if I would spend an hour or two a day with the Lord, things would be well with me, I took God at His word. I began to get up an hour earlier in the morning, so I could spend time with Him before I began my day. When I started, it was wintertime. My alarm clock would go off and my flesh would say, "You don't want to get up. It's too dark! It's too cold!" My bed would feel so wonderful and warm that there were a few mornings during the first few weeks that I would agree with my body and go back to sleep.

I didn't let that stop me though. If I became lazy and went back to sleep, I would repent. Then I just asked God to help me, and the next morning I would go at it again! Eventually, my body became trained.

Your body can be trained to follow God just like it can be trained to follow the devil. Hebrews 5:14 says that mature believers have their "senses and mental faculties . . . trained by practice to discriminate and distinguish between . . . good and . . . evil" (AMP). If you practice the things of God, your body will eventually begin to cooperate with your spirit.

For a while, getting up earlier was a challenge for me. But, eventually, my body learned it wouldn't receive that extra hour of sleep anymore and it stopped complaining. It became accustomed to getting up earlier. I also believe for supernatural rest when I have a short night. It works!

The decision to make time for God every day has been one of the most important decisions of my life. It has made such a difference in my spiritual growth. I am not the same person I was then. People are always talking about how timid and restrained I used to be. I really was too, but I got over it!

Become Addicted to Jesus

By implementing the changes God instructed me to make, I created a lifestyle of communing with God. I became addicted to spending time with Him. Do you know what the word *addicted* means? It means "to devote, to deliver over, to apply habitually."

You can create good habits in God the same way you can create poor habits. If you will habitually apply yourself to spending time with Him daily, it will become a way of life for you. You won't even have to think about doing it. It will just come naturally to you.

That's what happened to me. I have developed such a habit of making time with God my first priority that I don't have to get up every day and think, *Well, should I pray this morning?* I just do it automatically. Now it is a way of life for me to spend the first part of my day in prayer. Even when Ken and I are traveling, even when I have to get up at four o'clock in the morning to do it—I do it.

You might think that's extreme. You might think I'm the only one around who is that committed to spending time with the Lord every day, but I'm not. I'm just one of many.

I have one friend in particular who is very diligent about it. Her name is Dodie Osteen. No matter how early she has to get up in the morning, no matter what else her schedule may hold, she puts her time in the Word and in prayer first place in her day. That's because many years ago she found herself dying of liver cancer. The doctors had diagnosed it and told her she had only a few months to live.

Medical science couldn't help her, so she turned to God's medicine. She began to spend time reading and meditating on scriptures about healing each and every day. As a result, she is alive and well today with no trace of cancer in her body.

My friend knows she owes her very life to God's Word, so she is still faithful and diligent to partake of those scriptures and fellowship with God first thing every morning. She and her husband are ministers of the gospel and, like Ken and me, they often begin their days very early. But she says, "Even if I have to get up at 3:00 in the morning, I'll do it."

Certainly such faithfulness requires time and effort. It's not easy. But if believers fully understood the blessings it brings, they too would be willing to do whatever is necessary in order to make their time with God first priority every day.

There are great rewards for that kind of faithfulness! The Bible says, "For the eyes of the Lord run to and fro throughout the whole earth, to show himself strong in the behalf of them whose heart is perfect toward him" (2 Chronicles 16:9). *Perfect* there doesn't mean "without a flaw." To have a perfect heart is to be "faithful, loyal, dedicated and devoted."

God will pass over a million people to find that one who is loyal to Him. He scans the earth looking for a person who will put Him first and let Him be God in his life.

God wants to help us. He wants to move in our behalf. He wants to meet our every need and work miracles for us. If you were God, wouldn't you do that? Wouldn't you move in the lives of your children? The Bible says that if men know how to give good gifts to their children, how much more willing is our heavenly Father to give the Holy Spirit to His children. (See Luke 11:13.)

Well, we are God's children. We have been born of His Spirit. We look just like God on the inside, because He is our Father.

He has us in His heart. He cares about us. He loves each and every one of us as if we were each His only child. God has a great and wonderful ability to have a family of many millions, while treating each member as if he or she was the only one.

But God can't bless us like He wants to if we won't let Him be God in our lives. He can't pour out His provision upon us if we keep clogging up our heavenly supply line by putting other things before Him. He is restrained by our capacity to receive. If He is to show Himself strong on our behalf, our hearts will have to be turned wholly toward Him.

Your Desire Follows Your Attention

Maybe today your heart isn't turned wholly toward God. Maybe you're facing the same situation I was facing back in 1977. You have grown busy and lost your appetite for the things of God. You know you ought to be praying more and spending more time in the Word, but you've lost your desire. You just don't want to do it.

If so, you can turn yourself around. You can rekindle your fire for the Lord by making the same kinds of changes I made. Before long, you will find yourself addicted to God instead of the earthly pursuits that have been consuming you.

How can I be so sure?

Because God showed me that your desire always follows your attention. Most people think it's the other way around. They think their attention follows their desire, but that's not the case.

One of the greatest practical examples of this fact is the average golfer. In the springtime when the weather is nice and there is plenty of opportunity to play golf, most avid golfers become very absorbed in their sport. The more they play, the more they want to play. They think about it, read about it, talk about it. They are constantly wanting to play golf!

But when winter comes, they put away their golf clubs. They

stop talking about it and thinking about it. They don't mope around all winter because they can't be on the golf course. Why? Because they have turned their attention to other things, and their desire for golf has waned.

I have seen that same principle at work in our conventions. People will come to a Believers' Convention, and when they arrive they will often be completely caught up in natural affairs. They will be preoccupied, worrying and fussing about some business deal at the office or some problem they left at home.

But after just a day or two of attending the meetings and spending hours on end in the Word of God, they'll completely forget about that business deal and that problem. They will be so absorbed in the Word that those things don't seem so important.

It doesn't matter how disinterested you may have grown about the things of God. If you will turn your attention toward Him, your desire will follow.

I know that from experience. I turned my attention to the Word of God, spent time listening to tapes and spent time in prayer until I became so addicted to the things of God that I lost interest in many of the other things that had so engaged me before. For example, I enjoy interior decorating, and I used to spend a great deal of time at it. But as I became more involved in the things of God, I just didn't want to spend time in design anymore. Now it's a chore to do that.

Even today when I think about taking up some new project, starting a new hobby or buying something that would require me to spend my time maintaining it, I say to myself, *Can I afford this? Can I afford the time it will cost me?* Usually I decide I can't! I have come to value the things of God so much and have such great desire for them that I just don't want to give my time to anything else unless it is absolutely necessary.

Today I can give testimony that what I'm telling you is true. It has worked. At the writing of this book, everything is good in my life and in the lives of my family. Things are well with us. My children and grandchildren are healthy, blessed and serving the Lord.

There is no question about it. The time I've spent with God has changed my life. And I can say with certainty that if you will spend an hour or two a day with Him, it will change your life too.

How could it be otherwise? How could you possibly spend an hour or two daily with the highest authority and the kindest, most loving being in the universe without having it affect your life and future?

You may be facing problems today that seem to have no solutions. You may be caught in impossible circumstances. But I want you to know that God can change those things. If you will give Him a way into your life by fellowshiping with Him every day, He will give you a way out of those impossible circumstances. He will help you solve those problems. He will move on your behalf until you too can say, "All is well with me!"

If you want a change, make a change. Commit yourself to do whatever it takes to stay in right relationship with God, abide in Him and spend time with Him every day. Determine right now that by the strength and grace of God, if you have to get up earlier in the morning, you will do it. If you have to go to bed later at night, you will do it. If you have to change jobs, you will do it.

Decide no matter what it takes, you will maintain your communion with God; you will guard your heart above all, for out of it flow the issues of life.

Agree with me now as I pray for you.

Father, thank You for revealing to us the wonderful fact that we can fellowship with You. Thank You for reminding us that we can spend time with You and talk to You. It is such a great blessing to know You'll give us wisdom and reveal to us in every situation what we should do and then give us help and strength from Your Spirit to carry it through.

I pray for the person who is reading this book right now, Lord. I pray that You will quicken within them a great desire to go on in the things of God, to go on in the walk of faith, to increase spiritually more and more. Give this person such a strong desire that it will overcome all laziness, every distraction and every hindrance that has held them back from spending time with You.

In the Name of Jesus, I break the power of the enemy over this precious believer. I release this person in Jesus' Name from any spirit of lethargy. I release the power of God right now to rise up within and come upon and to endue this believer with power, Lord, so they can go on and do the things they purpose to do in their heart. Give this person the power and the grace to go on and increase and to not draw back or be lazy.

Strengthen this person out of the rich treasury of Your glory, Lord, with might in the inner man. Enable them to rise up and become on fire for You, to march forward and do the things necessary to maintain this person's time and union with You at all costs.

We know, Father, that in the end it won't cost us, it will pay us. It will bless us. It might cause a little harassment on our flesh for a while, but the Bible says we have been crucified with Christ and that flesh has to be put under subjection. We know we cannot do that in our own strength. So we depend on You, fully confident that You will help us, encourage us and enable us to do what we know to do.

Now reveal to those who read these words exactly what they need to do in order to grow and maintain their spiritual walk. Show them what they need to drop out of their lives and what they need to add. Give them spiritual goals they can set to help them walk in the spirit. Teach them to maintain a lifestyle of daily fellowshiping with You.

We give You all the praise, Lord. In Jesus' Name. Amen.

Notes

1 Kenneth S. Wuest, *Wuest's Word Studies from the Greek New Testament,* Vol. I [Grand Rapids: Wm. B. Eerdmans Publishing Co., 1973] p. 163.

2 *The Fruit of the Spirit,* Donald Gee [Springfield: Gospel Publishing House, 1928], p. 60, used by permission of publisher.

3 Romans 12:1, Kenneth S. Wuest, *An Expanded Translation* [Grand Rapids: Wm. B. Eerdmans Publishing Co., 1961].

4 "Lord, Lordship," W.E. Vine, *Vine's Expository Dictionary of Biblical Words* [Nashville: Thomas Nelson Publishers, 1985], p. 379.

5 J. Rufus Moseley, *Manifest Victory, A Quest and a Testimony* [Saint Paul: Macalester Park Publishing Co., Reprinted 1986], p. 121.

6 J. Rufus Moseley, *Manifest Victory, A Quest and a Testimony* [Saint Paul: Macalester Park Publishing Co., 1986], p. 117.

7 *John G. Lake—His Life, His Sermons, His Boldness of Faith,* rev. ed. [Fort Worth: Kenneth Copeland Publications, 1994], p. 59.

8 *The Companion Bible* (Grand Rapids: Kregel Publications, 1990), p. 892.

9 "Tongues," meaning not their own language, but an unknown language given by the Holy Spirit.

10 Noah Webster, *An American Dictionary of the English Language* [New York: S. Converse, 1828], "diligent."

11 *John G. Lake—His Life, His Sermons, His Boldness of Faith,* rev. ed. [Fort Worth: Kenneth Copeland Publications, 1994], pp. 9–10.

12 John G. Lake's sermons have been compiled into the book *John G. Lake—His Life, His Sermons, His Boldness of Faith,* which is available through Kenneth Copeland Ministries, Fort Worth, Texas 76192-0001.

Prayer for Salvation and Baptism in the Holy Spirit

Heavenly Father, I come to You in the Name of Jesus. Your Word says, "Whosoever shall call on the name of the Lord shall be saved" (Acts 2:21). I am calling on You. I pray and ask Jesus to come into my heart and be Lord over my life according to Romans 10:9–10: "If thou shalt confess with thy mouth the Lord Jesus, and shalt believe in thine heart that God hath raised him from the dead, thou shalt be saved. For with the heart man believeth unto righteousness; and with the mouth confession is made unto salvation." I do that now. I confess that Jesus is Lord, and I believe in my heart that God raised Him from the dead.

I am now reborn! I am a Christian—a child of Almighty God! I am saved! You also said in Your Word, "If ye then, being evil, know how to give good gifts unto your children: HOW MUCH MORE shall your heavenly Father give the Holy Spirit to them that ask him?" (Luke 11:13). I'm also asking You to fill me with the Holy Spirit. Holy Spirit, rise up within me as I praise God. I fully expect to speak with other tongues as You give me the utterance (Acts 2:4). In Jesus' Name. Amen!

Begin to praise God for filling you with the Holy Spirit. Speak those words and syllables you receive—not in your own language, but the language given to you by the Holy Spirit. You have to use your own voice. God will not force you to speak. Don't be concerned with how it sounds. It is a heavenly language!

Continue with the blessing God has given you and pray in the spirit every day.

You are a born-again, Spirit-filled believer. You'll never be the same!

Find a good church that boldly preaches God's Word and obeys it. Become a part of a church family who will love and care for you as you love and care for them.

We need to be connected to each other. It increases our strength in God. It's God's plan for us.

Make it a habit to watch the *Believer's Voice of Victory* television broadcast and become a doer of the Word, who is blessed in his doing (James 1:22–25).

Questions for Reflection and Discussion

CHAPTER 1: FIRST THINGS FIRST

1. Why is staying in daily communion with God the Christian's number one priority?
2. What happens to Christians who try to serve God in their own strength? Have you ever done this? What happened?
3. What does it mean to "abide with God"?
4. How did God make it possible for believers to "come boldly unto the throne of grace"?
5. How can you begin to make a living connection with Jesus today?

CHAPTER 2: LIVING TO KNOW HIM

1. Why is it "just plain smart" to spend time with God daily?
2. What is the key to victory in life? Are you currently using this "key"?
3. Why should you seek God in good times as well as bad?
4. During a difficult time, have you ever persevered in faith? What happened?
5. Are you in the midst of a good time or a bad time? Are you seeking God?

CHAPTER 3: SURPRISE! GOD IS GOOD— NOT ANGRY

1. Describe the picture you had of God before you read this chapter. Has it changed?
2. What has God treasured up for each of His children?
3. Why can you be sure that God hears you?
4. What does 1 Corinthians 13 reveal about God's love for *you*?
5. Are you growing in your knowledge that "God is love"? If not, how can you increase your faith in this fact?

CHAPTER 4: ABIDING IN THE VINE

1. What does it mean to "abide" in Jesus?
2. What things cause you to lose your connection with the Vine? Are any of those things disrupting your spiritual communion now?
3. Are you bearing "much fruit" in your spiritual life right now? Why or why not?
4. Why do some prayers seem to go unanswered?
5. Do you find the Christian life simple—or impossible? What makes the difference?

CHAPTER 5: IT'S MORE THAN POSSIBLE— IT'S INEVITABLE!

1. How is joy more than a nice feeling? How can it help you spiritually?

2. Are you experiencing "days of heaven upon the earth"? If not, what can you do to change that?

3. Describe what it means to be faithful to the Word of God.

4. Is freedom usually an instant result of becoming saved? What does Ephesians 4:22–24 tell us about attaining freedom?

5. What two ways does communion with God through His Word cleanse you of sin?

CHAPTER 6: PLEASING THE FATHER

1. Can God fulfill His will for your life without your cooperation? What did Abraham have to do to see God's plan fleshed out in his life?

2. What must you do to see the power of God manifested in your life? What did Jesus do?

3. What assurance do you have that you can please God as much as Jesus did?

4. What is the difference between righteousness and holiness?

CHAPTER 7: A LIVING SACRIFICE

1. What kinds of things draw people away from God? What things draw *you* away from Him?

2. What three things must you do to move in the flow of the Holy Spirit?

3. Why is putting your body "at the disposal of God" a reasonable act of service?

4. As you submit to the Holy Spirit's leading, what will happen to the war between the flesh and the spirit?

5. How can you more fully submit to the Spirit today?

CHAPTER 8: KEEP THE UNION

1. What did the Apostle Paul mean when he wrote, "Let heaven fill your thoughts"?
2. What happens when you are "carnally minded"?
3. Are you, as a citizen of heaven, dependent on this world's economy? Describe its opposite, heaven's economy.
4. What does it mean to be "connected" with the God of the universe?
5. If you lived as if you were a conqueror, how would your life change?

CHAPTER 9: LET THE WORD ABIDE IN YOU

1. Why is it essential to have knowledge of the Word of God when you pray?
2. What will be the result if you pray for faith?
3. What happens if you read the Word just for knowledge or facts? What happens when you put words from the Bible in your heart?
4. What is your area of greatest need? What verses can you read and say out loud daily to help meet this need?
5. Have you ever gone on a "Word binge"? Do you need to?

CHAPTER 10: ABIDING IS OBEYING

1. How did God respond to Jesus' obedience to the Word? Do you long for this same result in your life?

2. What kind of life will obedience to God's Word bring?
3. What did Rufus Moseley discover to be the "master key of the Kingdom of Heaven"? Do you use this key?
4. When you live in and express the "God kind of love," what happens to your behavior?
5. How can you develop an overcoming lifestyle?

CHAPTER 11: DEVELOPING CONFIDENCE IN THE HOLY SPIRIT

1. How have you viewed the Holy Spirit in your walk with Christ? Have you felt for Him an "awesome appreciation"?
2. What does the Holy Spirit do that Jesus, in the flesh, could not?
3. List five ways the Holy Spirit helps you.
4. What is "spiritual laziness"? Have you ever been guilty of it?
5. Are you "build[ing] your life in such a way that you can hear from heaven for yourself"? If not, how can you begin to do so today?

CHAPTER 12: DRAWING FROM GOD'S WISE COUNSEL

1. Why is the counsel of God "precious"? What does it bring to those who pursue it?
2. What does it mean to draw out divine counsel?
3. How does the Holy Spirit bring light to your life?

4. What can enable you to walk in victory when turmoil is all around you? Give an example of what this looks like.
5. What can "snuff out the candle of our spirit"? What habits or behaviors dim your "light" as a believer in Christ?

CHAPTER 13: WELLSPRINGS AND RIVERS— RECEIVING THE FULLNESS OF THE HOLY SPIRIT

1. What two experiences of the Holy Spirit are available to all believers? Have you experienced either of these?
2. Why does God want you to be overflowing with the Holy Spirit?
3. Why is the Baptism of the Holy Spirit an essential part of your ability to minister?
4. Why do all Christians need the gift of speaking in tongues?
5. Who can receive the Baptism of the Holy Spirit—is anyone eligible?

CHAPTER 14: STAYING CONNECTED TO HEAVEN

1. What are the three ways to develop discernment so you can hear the Holy Spirit's voice?
2. How can you stay connected to the "realm of the spirit" throughout your day?
3. Do you need special abilities in order for God to work in and through you? What kind of person is God likely to seek out for His work?

4. Do you start your day dependent on the Holy Spirit? If not, how can you begin to do that?

5. How did the way Jesus lived reveal His dependence on the Holy Spirit?

CHAPTER 15: EXPECT TO BE LED BY THE SPIRIT

1. Have you ever heard the Spirit of God speak to you? Describe that experience.

2. Have you sensed the Holy Spirit's prompting to do something unusual? Describe.

3. What are some steps you can take to maintain your communion with the Holy Spirit?

4. Why is reasoning a mistake when the Holy Spirit is speaking to you?

5. Do you ever hesitate to obey from fear of looking foolish? How can you begin to let go of that fear?

CHAPTER 16: PRINCIPLES OF DIVINE DIRECTION

1. What does it mean to "roll your works upon the Lord"? Is this hard or easy for you? Why?

2. Have you ever sensed God giving you His thoughts? When?

3. What is to act as "umpire" when you are making decisions? Do you practice doing this?

4. How is being irritable a barrier to hearing from the Spirit of God?

5. Is your sense of peace fragile? How can you fight to keep your peace?

CHAPTER 17: GUARD YOUR HEART

1. What fills your heart today: cares and anxieties, or the things of God?
2. How can you keep your heart full of divine fullness?
3. If you sow to the spirit, what things will you reap?
4. What are some ways to "deposit" the Word in your heart?
5. Why is diligence vital to your walk with God?

CHAPTER 18: PRESSING IN—IT'S WORTH IT ALL

1. How determined are you to win the spiritual race? Are you pressing in? If not, why?
2. Why is a person's ability or intellect unimportant in the job God has for her?
3. Have you found that "when you're in God, you're over your head all the time"? Describe.
4. What is your "determined purpose"? In what ways are you pursuing it?
5. Do you "count your life dear unto yourself"? How do you know?

CHAPTER 19: IF YOU WANT A CHANGE, MAKE A CHANGE

1. Does desperation drive you to spend more time with God, or does worry drive you away from God?
2. Have you ever become lazy about the things of God? What did you do to rekindle your spiritual fire?

3. Have you begun to make time for God every day? If not, how can you begin forming that habit?

4. What prevents God's blessings from flowing in your life? What is the remedy?

5. How has time spent with God changed your life so far? How do you expect your communion with Him to change you in the future?

About the Author

Gloria Copeland is a noted author and minister of the gospel whose teaching ministry is known throughout the world. Believers worldwide know her through Believers' Conventions, Victory Campaigns, magazine articles, teaching audios and videos, and the daily and Sunday *Believer's Voice of Victory* television broadcast, which she hosts with her husband, Kenneth Copeland. She is known for "Healing School," which she began teaching and hosting in 1979 at KCM meetings. Gloria delivers the Word of God and the keys to victorious Christian living to millions of people every year.

Gloria has written many books, including *God's Will for You, Walk With God, God's Will Is Prosperity, Hidden Treasures, Living Contact,* and *Are You Listening?* She has also co-authored several books with her husband, including *Family Promises, Healing Promises,* and the best-selling daily devotionals, *From Faith to Faith* and *Pursuit of His Presence.*

She holds honorary doctorates from Oral Roberts University, Miami Bible Institute, and Life Christian University. In 1994, Gloria was voted Christian Woman of the Year, an honor conferred on women whose example demonstrates outstanding Christian leadership. Gloria is also the co-founder and vice president of Kenneth Copeland Ministries in Fort Worth, Texas.

Learn more about
Kenneth Copeland Ministries
by visiting our Web site
at **www.kcm.org.**

World Offices of
Kenneth Copeland Ministries

For more information about KCM and a free catalog, please write
the office nearest you:

Kenneth Copeland Ministries
Fort Worth, Texas 76192-0001

Kenneth Copeland
Locked Bag 2600
Mansfield Delivery Centre
QUEENSLAND 4122
AUSTRALIA

Kenneth Copeland
Post Office Box 15
BATH
BA1 3XN
U.K.

Kenneth Copeland
Private Bag X 909
FONTAINEBLEAU
2032
REPUBLIC OF
SOUTH AFRICA

Kenneth Copeland
Post Office Box 3111
STN LCD #1
Langley, B.C. V3A 4R3
CANADA

Kenneth Copeland Ministries
Post Office Box 84
L'VIV 79000
UKRAINE

We're Here for You!

Believer's Voice of Victory
Television Broadcast

Join Kenneth and Gloria Copeland and the *Believer's Voice of Victory* broadcasts Monday through Friday and on Sunday each week, and learn how faith in God's Word can take your life from ordinary to extraordinary. This teaching from God's Word is designed to get you where you want to be—on top! You can catch the *Believer's Voice of Victory* broadcast on your local, cable or satellite channels. Check your local listings for times and stations in your area.

Believer's Voice of Victory
Magazine

Enjoy inspired teaching and encouragement from Kenneth and Gloria Copeland and guest ministers each month in the *Believer's Voice of Victory* magazine. Also included are real-life testimonies of God's miraculous power and divine intervention into the lives of people just like you!

It's more than just a magazine—it's a ministry.

To receive a FREE subscription to
Believer's Voice of Victory, write:

Kenneth Copeland Ministries
Fort Worth, Texas 76192-0001

Or call: (800) 600-7395 (7 a.m.–5 p.m. CT)
Or visit our Web site at: www.kcm.org

If you are writing from outside the U.S., please contact the KCM office nearest you. Addresses for all Kenneth Copeland Ministries offices are listed on page 209.